D0893453

IRAN: THE KHOMEINI REVOLUTION

IRAN: THE KHOMEINI REVOLUTION

COUNTRIES IN CRISIS

Edited by
MARTIN WRIGHT

**Contributors: Nick Danziger, Martin Howe,
Baqer Moin, Reza Navabpour, Sir Anthony Parsons,
Vahe Petrossian, Amit Roy and Martin Wright**

StJ

ST. JAMES PRESS
CHICAGO AND LONDON

IRAN: THE KHOMEINI REVOLUTION

Published by Longman Group UK Limited,
Westgate House, The High, Harlow, Essex CM20 1YR, UK.
Telephone (0279) 442601
Telex 817484
Facsimile (0279) 444501

Published in the United States and Canada by St James Press,
233 East Ontario St, Chicago 60611, Illinois, U.S.A.

ISBN 0-582-04444-8 (Longman, hard cover)
0-582-04443-X (Longman, paper cover)
1-55862-015-X (St James)

First published in 1989

British Library Cataloguing in Publication Data
Wright, Martin, *1958–*
    Iran: the Khomeini revolution.—(Countries
    in crisis)
    1. Iran. Political events
    I. Title   II. Series
    955'.054

    ISBN 0–582–04444–8
    ISBN 0–582–04443–X Pbk

Printed in Great Britain by Bell and Bain Ltd., Glasgow

CONTENTS

ABOUT THE AUTHORS

Nick Danziger is a writer and photographer who has travelled widely in Iran, Afghanistan and elsewhere. He is the author of *Danziger's Travels* (Grafton Books, 1987).

Martin Howe is a freelance writer and television producer, currently working on Channel 4's international current affairs programme, *The World This Week*. He has contributed articles on Middle Eastern affairs to *Keesing's Record of World Events* and was formerly with the BBC World Service.

Baqer Moin is a specialist on Iran and Islam who works for the BBC World Service in London. His biography of Ayatollah Khomeini is due to be published later this year.

Reza Navabpour graduated from Tehran University and is currently attached to the Centre for Middle Eastern and Islamic Studies at the University of Durham. He has recently completed a Ph.D thesis on Iranian society and literature, and a *Bibliography of Iran* (Clio Press, 1988).

Sir Anthony Parsons served as British Ambassador to Iran from 1974 to 1979. He was subsequently Ambassador to the United Nations, and adviser on foreign affairs to the Prime Minister. He has written widely on Iranian and Middle Eastern affairs.

Vahe Petrossian is on the staff of the *Middle East Economic Digest*. He is a frequent visitor to Iran and has contributed articles on the country to a number of newspapers.

Amit Roy is senior features writer at *The Sunday Times* and has visited Tehran on numerous occasions since the revolution. He was previously *Daily Telegraph* staff correspondent in Tehran in 1979–81.

Martin Wright is editor of the *Countries in Crisis* series. Formerly on the staff of *Keesing's Record of World Events*, he now works as a publishing consultant and freelance journalist, and has travelled widely through the Middle East, Africa and Asia. He is the editor of *Revolution in the Philippines* (Longman, 1988).

PREFACE

Ten years after the revolution which swept Ayatollah Khomeini into power and the Shah into history's dustbin, the Islamic Republic of Iran has emerged from its ruinous war with Iraq to find itself facing mounting economic problems and a divided leadership. Without the unifying influence of an external threat, the government is faced with the major tasks of reconstructing its economy and rebuilding public confidence. Despite these problems, however, the future of the regime looks fairly secure, with precious little internal opposition and its exiled opponents divided and discredited.

This book provides a detailed, readable account of the events leading up to the revolution and of the first ten, turbulent years of Khomeini's rule. Part I provides a brief historical survey of medieval Persia's transition into modern Iran, of the Shah's *coup d'état* and his "White Revolution" of modernization, and the rise of the broad-based opposition in the late 70s. It gives a detailed account of the Islamic revolution, showing how the fundamentalists emerged triumphant, and of the political shifts and balances in the 1980s. Other chapters chart Iran's fluctuating fortunes in the Gulf War, and its relations with the outside world, including the twin dramas of the seizure of the US embassy in 1979, and the revelations of the "arms-for-hostages" affair eight years later.

In Part II, leading commentators examine some of the critical issues facing the Islamic Republic, and reveal some of the reasons and motivation behind its often alarming or contradictory actions and policies. The Reportage features look behind the mask of politics to give a glimpse of the impact of events and radical change on everyday life in Iran.

Acknowledgements The Editor wishes to extend his thanks to the *Middle East Journal* (1761 N St NW, Washington DC, 20036–0162) for permission to include the briefing by Sir Anthony Parsons, and to Roger East, Frances Nicholson and Neil Hicks for their advice and support at various stages of the project.

The front cover photograph, by Moradabadi, was provided by Reflex Picture Agency. Permission for the use of this photograph and others appearing within the text by K. Golestan (for Reflex), and by Nick Danziger, is gratefully acknowledged. Copyright remains with the Agency/photographers. Thanks are also due to CARPRESS International Press Agency for providing the map on p. viii.

IRAN: INFRASTRUCTURE

The Islamic Republic of Iran has an area of 165 million hectares and is bordered in the north by the USSR, in the west by Turkey and Iraq, in the east by Afghanistan and Pakistan and in the south by the Persian (Arab) Gulf and the Gulf of Oman. The country is made up of an interior plateau, 1,000 metres to 1,500 metres above sea-level, surrounded on almost all sides by mountains. Most of the cultivatable land is situated in or near the foothills of these mountains as the central plateau is largely salt swamp and areas of loose sand and stones. The climate is one of extremes. In the summer temperatures can reach as high as 55°C, but in the winter the altitude of the country causes temperatures to drop to below –20°C. Much of Iran is arid, but the north and north-west has a hot humid climate with considerable rainfall, which has made it the most densely populated region.

The population of Iran in the 1986 census was 49,857,384. The main language is Farsi (Persian), spoken by approximately half the people. Turkic-speaking Azerbaijanis make up a further 27 per cent and Kurds, Arabs, Turkomans and Baluchis comprise less than 25 per cent. Most of the Persians and Azerbaijanis belong to a minority branch of Islam called the Shia (about 10–15 per cent of the world's Moslems belong to this branch of Islam), while the other ethnic groups are mainly Sunnis. There are also small minorities of Christians, Jews and Zoroastrians.

The topography and climate have restricted the land under cultivation to around 10 per cent of the total area and the bulk of this is in the north. Agriculture is still the leading employer, but people are moving away from the rural areas into the towns in search of work and on present trends Iran will have only a quarter of its population in the countryside by 1990. The chief crops are grains (including wheat, barley and rice), cotton, sugar-beet, almonds, pistachios and dates. Away from the towns and cultivated areas most of the population, between three and four million people, live as animal-herding nomads.

Iran has large petroleum deposits, estimated in 1987 to be at least 93,000 barrels, situated mainly in the south-west of the country. Production was severely disrupted by the Islamic revolution and by the Gulf War, but oil sales account for approximately 80 per cent of government revenue and about 95 per cent of foreign exchange earnings. Iran has the second largest deposits of natural gas in the world, and substantial deposits of copper, iron ore and coal.

The country's main industries are steel, petrochemicals and copper, followed by car–manufacturing, machine tools, construction materials, pharmaceuticals, textiles and food processing.

The development of communications in Iran has been restricted by the terrain. A railway link was built before the Second World War between the Caspian coast, Tehran and the Persian Gulf, and since the mid-sixties a network of roads has been constructed linking the main cities.

PART I: HISTORICAL SURVEY

IRAN BEFORE KHOMEINI

Iran (known as Persia up to 1935) has a history stretching back 2,500 years. Founded by Cyrus the Great in 533 BC, the first Iranian empire covered present-day Turkey, the eastern Mediterranean and Egypt. The empire was overthrown by Alexander the Great in 331 BC and for the next thousand years Iran, or parts of it, were fought over by a series of imperial powers. When the last empire of the Sassanians was defeated by Arab Moslems at the Battle of Qadisiyya in AD 637, Iran was absorbed into the Moslem world. By the ninth century most Iranians, previously Zoroastrian, had converted to Islam and in the sixteenth century Shi'ism was declared the state religion. This set Iran apart from its Sunni neighbours, the Ottoman Turks, and helped create a united, independent nation with boundaries similar to those of today.

The first significant contacts with European countries, from the late sixteenth century onwards, were initially based on the trade in silk. However, European strategic ambitions centering on Iran soon became apparent. For Russia, Iran formed a potential part of its imperial expansion southwards, while Britain was concerned to protect the land route to India. This led the independence of the Qajar dynasty (1796–1925), to be progressively compromised. It owed its existence and authority to Russia and Britain, who throughout the nineteenth and first half of the twentieth centuries competed for commercial and strategic advantage.

Their growing influence, together with the increasing extravagance of the Shah's court, led to numerous favourable trading concessions being granted, ranging from transport networks to the exploitation of mineral resources. Opposition to these concessions was largely orchestrated by the Moslem clergy. As the Shah continued to grant concessions, demands for reform grew in strength. In August 1906, following a series of strikes, the then Shah, Muzaffar al-Din, finally agreed to introduce a Constituent National Assembly, or *Majlis*, and a constitution. This step down the constitutionalist path was undermined by the Anglo-Russian agreement of 1907. The agreement divided the country into three zones of influence: Russian in the north, British in the south and a neutral zone in between, and was seen by many Iranians as reducing the country to semi-colonial status.

In June 1908 Mohammed Ali Shah staged a *coup d'état* against the government. His Cossack Brigade bombed the National Assembly, dissolved the *Majlis* and declared martial law. Civil war broke out and the Shah was forced to abdicate in 1909. The second *Majlis* met later that year and attempted to solve the economic problems facing the country by appointing an American, Mr W. M. Schuster, as Treasurer-General. The Russians, with the backing of the British, demanded his dismissal in November 1911. The cabinet relented, the *Majlis* was dissolved and Mr Schuster dismissed in December. The *Majlis* did not meet again until 1914.

During the First World War Iran was officially neutral, but German agents and British, Russian and Turkish forces were active in the country and by the end of the war Iran was in chaos. In 1920 a short-lived Autonomous Soviet Republic of Gilan was established in the north and the country appeared to be on the verge of division and collapse. However, Colonel Reza Khan, Commander of the Cossack Brigade, staged a *coup d'état* on Feb.20, 1921 and became Minister of War under a pro-British Prime Minister, Sayyed Zia al-Din. He took over all the security forces and successfully defeated the rebellions in Gilan and elsewhere. In October 1923 he became Prime Minister and in late 1925, after the *Majlis* voted to depose the Shah, he was crowned as Reza Shah Pahlavi in early 1926.

Reza Shah marked a turning point in Iranian history. He tried to make the country truly independent of all foreign powers and to radically transform Iran into a modern centralized state. He expanded the army and set up a national civil service, introduced a secular legal system, brought in Western-style education, established new dress codes that meant that women no longer had to wear the veil, encouraged Iranian industry, and improved communications. Reza Shah became an increasingly powerful authoritarian figure at odds with a growing opposition, particularly the clergy. In spite of all his nationalist rhetoric, Reza Shah was unable to end Iran's dependence on the West. During the 1930s Germany became increasingly important as a source of machinery and advice for the modernization programme. At the outbreak of World War Two, Reza Shah declared Iran's neutrality, but Great Britain and the USSR were suspicious of the number of Germans in the country and following the German invasion of the USSR, demanded a reduction in their numbers. Reza Shah hesitated and Britain and the USSR invaded in August 1941. The Shah abdicated in favour of his 22-year-old son, Mohammed Reza, and was deported to South Africa where he died in 1944.

The young Shah ushered in a new era in Iran. Political activity burgeoned and cabinet-led government was revived. Political parties sprung up; the (Marxist–Leninist) Tudeh Party was formed in 1941 and trade unions reappeared in 1942. However, the old problems remained: the country was occupied by foreign troops and the economy was in a state of collapse. In January 1942 Iran signed a Tripartite Treaty of Alliance with Great Britain and the USSR, which stated that Allied forces would withdraw not later than six months after the end of the war. As some form of guarantee, the Shah turned to the United States for assistance and US advisers were appointed to the army, gendarmerie and finance ministry. The economy, however, had been marred throughout the war by inflation and widespread shortages.

Central government authority, already weak, now faced widespread unrest, particularly in the tribal regions and the north-west of the country, where autonomous governments were set up in Azerbaijan in December 1945 and in Kurdistan in early 1946. Both had the active support of the USSR which used troops to prevent the Tehran authorities from suppressing the two governments. In March 1946 Great Britain and the USA withdrew their troops with the USSR only agreeing to do so under international pressure in May. Azerbaijan and Kurdistan were re-occupied by the Iranian army in late 1946 and Soviet influence declined. A number of agreements for military aid and assistance were signed with the USA in 1947 and 1948.

Internal unrest continued. In 1949 the Shah used an assassination attempt as a pretext for banning the Tudeh Party and clamping down on the political opposition. He attempted some economic reforms and introduced a Seven Year Plan, which aimed to improve agricultural output, but it failed to meet even its own modest targets and was effectively suspended after the oil crisis of 1951.

A long history of resentment over foreign involvement in the oil industry, particularly that of Great Britain (which had won the first oil concession in 1901 and established the Anglo-Iranian Oil Company in 1909) came to a head in 1951 when the *Majlis* voted through an Oil Nationalization Bill. The British instigated a world-wide boycott of Iranian oil, which was eventually supported by the United States. The loss of oil revenues and potential loans from the United States was a severe blow to the Iranian economy. Prime Minister Mohammed Mossadeq, leader of the National Front, sought increasing powers to deal with the crisis, which in turn brought him into conflict with the Shah, who was opposed to the nationalist independent stance of the Mossadeq administration. The economy continued to deteriorate, negotiations over an oil settlement were stalled and Dr Mossadeq was losing support from within his party, the National Front. Moves were set in train, supported and aided by the United States and Great Britain to remove Dr Mossadeq, and in August 1953 he was overthrown and replaced as Prime Minister by General Fazlollah Zahedi, a strong supporter of the Shah.

The Shah set about improving relations with the West and began to receive extensive military and financial aid from the United States. this taken together with revenue from a new oil agreement, in which Iran shared oil profits fifty-fifty with a consortium of eight international oil companies, revived the depressed economy. The Shah strengthened the armed forces and initiated a number of economic development plans, but this growing prosperity was bought at the cost of soaring inflation and growing corruption.

Internally, however, the Shah was looking increasingly secure. Most of the opposition was in disarray and was further emasculated by SAVAK, a secret police force established in 1957. He was, however, coming under pressure from the United States to introduce some reform to broaden his base of support, improve economic efficiency and reduce corruption. Accordingly in January 1963 he launched his "White Revolution", which amongst other things called for land reform and the emancipation of women. Opposition by the clergy led to protest riots in Qom and Tehran. It was during this campaign that Ayatollah Ruhollah Khomeini first came to national prominence, with his outspoken criticisms of the reforms and of the Shah. He was arrested a number of times during 1963 and 1964 before being exiled, first to Turkey and then to Iraq.

The White Revolution enjoyed some success and the Shah began to rule with growing self-confidence, taking a greater role in government. Parliamentary politics, which had been discredited by the rigging of elections in the early sixties, entered a period of stability. Amir Abbas Hoveida, a supporter of the Shah's reform programme, was elected Prime Minister in 1965 and remained in office until August 1977. Party politics continued to function and there were elections in 1967, 1971 and 1975. But in March 1975 the Shah announced that all legal parties should merge to form a single party—the Iran National Resurgence Party (*Rastakhiz*).

Throughout this period the Shah worked to build up the economy and strengthen his military and political ties with the West. Between 1963 and 1972 there were two ambitious five year plans, which continued his land reform programme and encouraged industrial development. The Shah's aim was for Iran to become one of the top five powers in this century and the mechanism for achieving this was oil. Oil revenues increased steadily throughout the 1960s and early 1970s, but following the OPEC oil price rise in the later part of 1973, behind which the Shah was a prime mover, oil income shot up dramatically.

The Shah had been presiding over an extensive military build-up since the late sixties. In January 1968 the British government announced its decision to

end its military commitments east of Suez by the end of 1971; both Great Britain
and the United States were happy to see the Shah take up the role of policeman of
the Gulf. President Richard Nixon relaxed US policy towards arms sales to Iran
by severing the link with internal reform. Military contracts with the USA rose
dramatically from around US$500 million in 1972 to US$2,500 million in 1973.

The arms budget distorted an economy already running into difficulties, resulting in shortages, soaring inflation and widespread corruption.
Western-style consumption among the wealthy together with a widening
income disparity between the rich and poor exacerbated discontent brought
about by urban overcrowding, high rents and land prices. The large number
of foreign technicians needed to make up the shortfall in skilled labour only
added fuel to the opposition's criticisms.

These grievances were voiced most effectively by the Moslem clergy, who
were opposed to the whole secular and Western nature of the Shah's modernization programme. They received much support from the urban poor and from
the merchants who were suffering from a series of anti-profiteering laws. The
Shah, remote and obsessed with his own vision of Iran, relied increasingly on
SAVAK to keep control over his opponents.

At the beginning of 1977, the Shah attempted to clean up his international
image, in part prompted by the human rights policy of newly-elected US
President Jimmy Carter. He released a number of political prisoners, opened
up the prisons to the International Red Cross and reined in SAVAK. Jamshed
Amuzegar was brought in as Prime Minister in an unsucessful attempt to solve
the economic crisis. A revived opposition, in particular the National Front and
Tudeh Party, began to take a more active role, while Ayatollah Khomeini
stepped up his criticisms from Iraq. In October, Khomeini's son died in
mysterious circumstances and in a number of cities there were clashes with
police following mourning processions. Those arrested were treated leniently
by the courts, but this was to be for the last time. After a visit to Washington in
November, the Shah, reassured of continued US support, ordered a stepped-up
campaign of repression against the opposition.

1978 — THE SHAH'S FINAL YEAR

President Carter visited Tehran on New Year's Eve 1977 and memorably
declared that "Iran under the great leadership of the Shah is an island of
stability". On Jan.7, 1978, a direct personal attack on Ayatollah Khomeini was
published in the newspaper, *Ettelaat*. It was believed to have been sanctioned
by the Shah himself. The result was one of the most violent demonstrations

since 1963 in Qom with an unspecified number of people killed when police opened fire on the crowds. The spark had been lit.

Ayatollah Khomeini immediately called for further demonstrations, all mosques in Tehran closed for a week and a strike was called for on Feb.18, marking the end of the traditional Islamic mourning period of 40 days for those killed. On that day, large mourning processions were held in Iran's main cities and markets and shops were closed. The majority passed off peacefully but in Tabriz rioting broke out and order was only restored two days after martial law was declared. Casualty figures varied between the official total of 12 people killed and opposition claims of over 100.

Ayatollah Khomeini spoke out in support of the demonstrators and this encouraged the call for a general strike on March 30, to coincide with the end of the 40-day mourning period for those killed in February. It took place against a background of anti-government demonstrations organized by the Moslem clergy throughout Iran. The most violent was at Yazd, where party officers, banks and cinemas were attacked, and 25 people were killed by the police.

The Iranian government was determined to end the violence, and at what was to be one of the last major demonstrations in support of the Shah, in Tabriz on April 9, it announced the setting up of armed "people's committees". Such measures had no real effect on the cycle of demonstrations which broke out afresh in towns across Iran on May 7, 40 days after the killings in Yazd. These marked a serious escalation of the protests for not only did they take place for the first time in the centre of Tehran, but they also involved the university students and communists, the first such public demonstration since the banning of the Tudeh Party in 1949.

The government offered concessions in an attempt to break the 40-day cycle of violence. The Shah banned pornographic films, ended a number of price-control restrictions, dismissed the head of SAVAK, General Nematollah Nasseri, and instructed members of the royal family to sever all business connections. These moves did indeed buy the regime some time. Ayatollah Seyyed Ghassem Shariatmadari (the senior Shia leader in Iran) called for peaceful demonstrations and the end of the next 40-day mourning period due on June 17 passed off uneventfully.

It was not to last. Violence broke out in Meshed on July 22 after the funeral of a prominent local cleric who had been killed in a car crash. Clashes with police and troops left over 40 dead. Many cities held seven-day mourning processions and serious unrest was reported at the beginning of August in Tehran, Qom, Tabriz and particularly Isfahan, where martial law was declared after 10 days of violence.

On Aug.5, the eve of Ramadan, the Shah addressed the nation and pledged that he would guarantee political liberties, such as freedom of the press, and that elections planned for June 1979 would be "100 per cent free". However, any hopes of accommodation between the two sides ended on August 19 when over 400 people, mainly women and children, burned to death in the Rex cinema in Abadan. The identity of the arsonists was unknown, but SAVAK was widely blamed. Serious rioting broke out in Abadan during mourning ceremonies on Aug.22–23 and the army was sent in. The Shah was forced to make further concessions. On Aug.27 he appointed Mr Jafar Sharif-Emami as Prime Minister of a "government of reconciliation", which immediately announced the establishment of a new ministry to deal with religious affairs, the restoration of the Moslem lunar calendar (which the Shah had replaced in 1976 with an Imperial Calendar), the closure of gambling casinos and the release from prison of a number of leading clerics.

These measures came too late. On Sept.4, at the end of the holy month of Ramadan, between 200,000 and 500,000 people marched through Tehran, demanding the return of Ayatollah Khomeini. The government imposed a ban on all opposition rallies, but this didn't stop a general strike and over 100,000 people marching through Tehran on Sept.7. Next day martial law was imposed for a period of six months in Tehran and 11 other cities. There were immediate demonstrations with the worst incident occurring at Jaleh, in the east of Tehran, when troops surrounded and shot at a crowd of around 5,000 young people. Estimates of the numbers killed during what the opposition called "Black Friday" varied from 97 to several thousand.

Throughout September the government tightened its grip on the opposition; censorship was reintroduced and the Iraqi government was persuaded to place Ayatollah Khomeini under virtual house arrest. On Oct. 6 he was expelled from Iraq, at the personal urging of the Shah, and moved to France. His expulsion proved to be a serious mistake as Khomeini now had access to the world media, which he used to good effect. The expulsion also led to violent demonstrations across Iran. The Shah attempted to appease the opposition by announcing a series of amnesties for political prisoners and opponents abroad, but his government was now facing a new and potentially more serious threat.

Strike action in the oil industry had begun on Sept.24, when about 10,000 workers stopped work. The government warned that strikers would be arrested and tried before military courts, but this didn't prevent strikes spreading to other sectors of industry and the civil service. Their demands were initially for higher wages and improved conditions, but they soon merged with the political demands of the opposition, to form a broad anti-Shah movement. There was a widely-supported strike on Oct.16 to commemorate the 40th day of mourning for those killed on "Black Friday", and strikes continued throughout the rest of the month.

In an attempt to defuse the crisis the Shah offered the post of Prime Minister in a provisional coalition government to Dr Karim Sanjabi, a leader of the National Front. He was in Paris holding talks with Ayatollah Khomeini and rejected the idea, saying instead that the National Front would be joining forces with Ayatollah Khomeini in an anti-Shah coalition, effectively ruling out any possibility of compromise between the opposition and the Shah.

The government was facing an ever-deepening crisis. Troops had been sent to the oil fields and the oil industry was at a virtual standstill, over 1,000,000 civil servants were on strike and there was serious rioting in Tehran. In an effort to regain control the Shah appointed the Chief of Staff, General Gholam Reza Azhari, as head of a military government.

General Azhari introduced a stringent anti-corruption campaign, while at the same time strictly enforcing martial law regulations. He had some limited success in getting striking oil workers back to work on Nov.13 after threatening mass dismissals. But tension was high and oil output remained severely disrupted.

Ayatollah Khomeini called for a halt to all oil exports and for continued demonstrations. On Nov.28 the government responded by banning all processions in major towns and cities during Moharram, a Moslem month of mourning, which was due to start on Dec.2, during which they expected renewed trouble. They were not to be proved wrong. There were widespread disturbances and extensive casualties, a walkout by oil workers and calls for a general strike. The Shah offered some concessions: he released political detainees and lifted the ban on processions. The result was two anti-Shah rallies attended by over a million people each in the centre of Tehran on Dec.10 and 11.

Alarmed, the Shah ordered the security forces to prevent any further demonstrations, but the disturbances continued and there were reports of growing indiscipline in the armed forces. In mid-December the Shah again approached leading secular opposition leaders about forming a civilian coalition government that would guarantee his position as a constitutional monarch, but they came to nothing.

On Dec.23 two oil executives were assassinated. There were mass resignations of oil workers and by Dec.26 industrial action had completely halted the export of crude oil. The government introduced fuel rationing, saying that they had less than a week's supply of oil left. With the economy in crisis and most civil servants on strike, the regime was effectively paralysed.

CHRONOLOGY OF PRE-KHOMEINI ERA

533 BC Achaemenid empire established by Cyrus the Great. Defeated by Alexander the Great in 331 BC.

637 Sassanian empire (224–651) defeated by Moslem Arabs at the Battle of Qadisiyya.

1501–1722 Safavid Kings. Ismail Safavi (1501–24) declared Shi'ism as the state religion.

1796–1925 Qajar dynasty. Period marked by rivalry between Great Britain and Russia in Iran.

1872 Baron de Reuter, a British subject, granted a 70-year monopoly over communications, irrigation works, telegraph, almost all minerals and customs duties. Cancelled in 1873.

1901 William Knox D'Arcy, a British subject, awarded the first oil concession. The Anglo-Iranian Oil Company was founded in 1909.

Aug.5, 1906 Muzaffar al-Din Shah agreed to the introduction of a Constituent National Assembly (or *Majlis*) and a constitution, based on the Belgian model.

Aug.31, 1907 Anglo-Russian agreement divided Iran into three zones of influence: Russian in the north, British in the south and a neutral zone in-between.

June 23, 1908 Mohammed Ali Shah dissolved the *Majlis*. Civil war ensued and he was forced to abdicate in July 1909.

June 4, 1920–1921 Autonomous Soviet Socialist Republic of Gilan.

Feb.20, 1921 Bloodless *coup d'état* led by Colonel Reza Khan.

Oct.28, 1923   Reza Khan became Prime Minister.

December 1925   *Majlis* voted to vest monarchy in Reza Khan, crowned Reza Shah Pahlavi early in 1926.

Aug.25, 1941   British and Soviet troops invaded Iran, following a demand that Reza Shah reduce the number of Germans in the country.

Sept.16, 1941   Reza Shah abdicated in favour of his 22-year-old son, Mohammed Reza.

Jan.29, 1942   Tripartite Treaty of Alliance signed with Great Britain and the USSR, which stated that all Allied forces would leave Iran six months after the end of the war.

December 1945   Autonomous government set up in Azerbaijan, followed by another in Kurdistan in early 1946. Both supported by Soviet Union. Overthrown in December 1946.

March 15, 1951   *Majlis* voted to nationalize the oil industry. Dr Mohammed Mossadeq, leader of the National Front (founded in 1949), became Prime Minister in April. International boycott of Iranian oil.

July 1952   Dr Mossadeq resigned after clashing with Shah over appointment of Minister of War. Recalled after demonstrations.

August 1953   Dr Mossadeq overthrown in an operation supported and aided by the United States and Great Britain. Replaced as Prime Minister by General Fazlollah Zahedi.

August 1954   A new oil agreement negotiated. Iran shared oil profits fifty-fifty with a consortium of eight international oil companies.

1957   SAVAK (*Sazman-i Ittili'at va Amniyat-i Kishvar*), an intelligence and security organization, established.

March 5, 1959   Defence agreement signed with United States.

Jan.6, 1963   "White Revolution" launched. A six-point plan, which included land reform, the emancipation of women and a literacy programme.

Nov.4, 1964 Ayatollah Ruhollah Khomeini exiled first to Turkey and then Iraq, for his opposition to the reform programme.

January 1968 British government announced decision to withdraw all troops from east of Suez by end of 1971. Shah took up role of policeman of Gulf.

Oct.15–17, 1971 Lavish celebration at Persepolis to mark 2,500 years of Iranian monarchy.

May 30–31, 1972 President Richard Nixon visited Tehran and gave the Shah unlimited access to all US military equipment, except nuclear weapons.

1973 OPEC oil price rise significantly boosted Iranian oil revenues.

June 13, 1975 Border treaty signed with Iraq. The increased cross border contact helped Khomeini spread his message.

March 1975 All legal political parties merged to form the Iran National Resurgence Party (*Rastakhiz*).

Jan.15, 1977 President Jimmy Carter took office in the United States and linked aid to human rights.

October 1977 The death of Ayatollah Khomeini's son led to mourning processions in Iran.

Dec.31, 1977–Jan.1, 1978 President Carter visited Tehran and publicly affirmed his faith in the Shah.

Jan.7, 1978 The *Ettelaat* newspaper published a personal attack on Khomeini which led to demonstrations in Qom. An unspecified number of people killed.

Feb.18, 1978 Large processions held in main cities to mark the fortieth day of mourning for those killed at Qom. Riots in Tabriz.

March 30, 1978 Strikes and demonstrations throughout Iran in commemoration of those killed in Tabriz.

April 9, 1978 The last major pro-government demonstration took place in Tabriz.

May 7, 1978 Riots in major cities, including for the first time the centre of Tehran and the universities.

June 17, 1978 Peaceful demonstrations took place following concessions by government and appeals by Moslem leaders in Iran.

July 22, 1978 Over 40 killed in riots in Meshed.

Aug.5, 1978 Shah addressed nation and promised to guarantee political liberties.

Aug.19, 1978 Rex cinema in Abadan burned to ground and over 400 people killed.

Aug.27, 1978 Mr Jafar Sharif-Emami appointed Prime Minister of a "government of reconciliation", committed to the Islamic faith.

Sept.4, 1978 200,000–500,000 people marched through Tehran demanding the return of Ayatollah Khomeini.

Sept.8, 1978 "Black Friday". Martial law declared for period of six months in Tehran and other major cities. Demonstrators were fired on by army. The worst incident was at Jaleh, in east Tehran, where many were killed.

Sept.24, 1978 10,000 oil workers on strike.

Oct.6, 1978 Ayatollah Khomeini expelled from Iraq to France.

Oct.16, 1978 Widely supported strike to commemorate the 40th day of mourning for those killed on "Black Friday".

October 1978 Shah's offer of post of Prime Minister to Dr Karim Sanjabi, leader of National Front, rejected. Announcement of anti-Shah alliance between National Front and Ayatollah Khomeini.

Nov.6, 1978 Chief of Staff, General Gholam Reza Azhari, appointed Prime Minister of military government.

Dec.10–11, 1978   Two peaceful anti-Shah rallies of over a million people each took place in the centre of Tehran.

THE REVOLUTION

THE SHAH'S LAST THROW: THE BAKHTIAR GOVERNMENT

Faced with the unprecedented extent of political opposition to his regime, the Shah, on Dec.29, 1978, turned to Dr Shapour Bakhtiar, a long-standing member of the main secular opposition organization, the National Front, to form a government. Bakhtiar's acceptance of the post was immediately denounced by Ayatollah Khomeini and the National Front, which expelled him from the movement.

A French-educated lawyer, Bakhtiar, then aged 63, had been a critic of the Shah since Mossadeq's government. While he had served prison sentences totalling five years for anti-Shah activities, he had generally been regarded as one of the regime's more moderate critics. He was a senior member of the influential Bakhtiar tribe of south-western Iran, which had traditionally supported the monarchy.

The new cabinet was composed mostly of middle-class technocrats with little history of active participation in politics. Both the Kurdish and Azerbaijani minorities were represented, but it did not include any members of leading secular or religious opposition groups. Its programme, as approved by the *Majlis* on Jan.16, 1979 by 149 votes to 49, included the abolition of martial law, the dissolution of SAVAK, release of political prisoners and punishment of human rights violators and corrupt officials, the lifting of press censorship, the legalization of political parties, a greater role for Moslem clerics in the drafting of legislation, an end to oil exports to Israel and South Africa, and a policy of support for the Palestinians.

Bills abolishing SAVAK and establishing legal procedures for "the prosecution of those responsible for all the misfortunes of the past 25 years" were approved by the *Majlis* on Feb.5 (i.e., shortly before the overthrow of the Bakhtiar government—see below).

Bakhtiar promised on Jan.3 that the Shah would leave the country "for a period of rest and holiday" after the new government had been installed, and that a "Regency Council" would be set up to rule in the monarch's absence. The Shah himself had on Jan.1 spoken of his wish for a period away from the country; he repeated this desire in an address to the new government on Jan.6, although aides stressed that he would leave for a vacation and medical treatment only, and could be expected to return in due course.

The two main strands of opposition within Iran both denounced the new administration. Ayatollah Khomeini warned on Jan.6 that obedience to the government was tantamount to "obedience to Satan"; he called on all government employees to refuse to obey the new ministers and to lock them out of ministry offices. The National Front on Jan.4 issued a statement condemning Bakhtiar's acceptance of the premiership as "a betrayal of our cause"; on Jan.9, Dr Sanjabi described the new administration as "a plot by opportunists".

Popular opposition to the Bakhtiar government manifested itself in violent demonstrations across the country. Several hundred people were killed in clashes between protesters and security forces in Qazvin, Shiraz and Rafsanjan. Repeated strikes paralysed shops, banks and offices. In an ominous indication of increasing dissent within the armed forces, soldiers fraternized with anti-Shah demonstrators in Tehran on Jan.13.

In spite of the ferocity of opposition to it, Bakhtiar's government did receive widespread support from among liberal politicians (representatives of the professional middle classes) and certain Moslem religious leaders on the moderate wing of the anti-Shah movement. Bakhtiar claimed that many others were giving the government their "silent support" by refraining from criticism. In particular, the Ayatollahs Shariatmadari, Golpayegani and Marashi Najafi declared their willingness to support the new administration.

In an effort to win liberal sympathy, Bakhtiar's government in its first two weeks of power eased curfew restrictions, lifted press censorship and freed over 1,000 political prisoners. On the economic front, the new government succeeded in persuading a majority of striking oil workers to return to their jobs, although these were in part responding to requests from Khomeini and the National Front for sufficient production to meet domestic needs. In one of his final acts as monarch, the Shah on Jan.9 ordered members of his family to surrender all their personal property to the Pahlavi Foundation "for the use of religious, educational, social and welfare bodies organized by the people and run by them". Ostensibly a charitable trust, the Foundation had in effect functioned as a means of extending the royal family's control over the economy through substantial holdings in key areas, and as a "conduit for rewards to supporters of the regime", according to a report in the *International Herald Tribune*.

FLIGHT OF THE SHAH — RETURN OF THE AYATOLLAH

The Shah left Iran for the last time on Jan.16, flying with his wife, the Empress Farah, to Aswan in Egypt, where President Sadat greeted them with full ceremonial honours. Their three children had left for the United States the previous day. Prior to leaving, the Shah expressed a hope that Dr Bakhtiar's government would be able "to make up for the past and also lay foundations for the future. To achieve this we will need co-operation and patriotism in the highest sense. Our economy must start again and the people must start their lives anew. I have nothing else to say except that I will fulfil my duties in the same spirit of patriotism".

Prior to the Shah's departure, on Jan.13, a nine-man Regency Council was formed under the chairmanship of Sayed Jalal Tehrani (a former cabinet minister noted for his loyalty to the Shah). Council members included Dr Bakhtiar and several other moderate monarchists, including the Chief of Staff, Gen. Abbas Qharabaghi, the speakers of the *Majlis* and the Senate, and the chairman of the National Iranian Oil Company, Mr Abdullah Entezam. Gen. Qharabaghi had taken over as Chief of Staff on Jan.4 from the infamous Gen. Oveissi, known as "the butcher of Tehran" for ordering troops to open fire on demonstrators in 1963. Oveissi was later shot dead in Paris in 1984. The Council was set up under Article 42 of the constitution, which provided for the temporary departure of the monarch from the country. It was empowered to dissolve parliament, call elections or establish a constituent assembly to bring about a transition to a new regime.

The rift between the government and the opposition was emphasized on Jan.13, when Ayatollah Khomeini announced the formation of a "Revolutionary Islamic Council" which would replace the "illegal government" and set up a provisional Islamic government to oversee elections to a constituent assembly. Khomeini affirmed that he would not play an active part in the government, but would give "general guidance". As eventually announced in November 1979, the Council membership included Ayatollah Hossein Ali Montazeri (Khomeini's son-in-law), Ayatollah Seyed Ali Khamenei and Mr Abolhassan Bani-Sadr (both future presidents), Hojatolislam Hashemi Ali Akbar Rafsanjani and Dr Bazargan.

News of the Shah's departure was greeted with mass celebrations in the streets of Iran's major towns and cities. Khomeini indicated immediately that his movement would not change its attitude towards the Bakhtiar government despite the Shah's flight, and he warned ministers, members of the Regency Council and MPs "to resign or be responsible for the consequences". In a series of statements issued from his Paris headquarters, the Ayatollah congratulated his followers for forcing the Shah's departure. He urged them to preserve public order and thereby win the respect of the armed forces, whom he called upon to "abandon" the Shah and join the movement for an Islamic republic. In the wake of the Shah's departure, the National Front, in particular Dr Mehdi Bazargan, tried unsuccessfully to mediate between Khomeini and the government, in an attempt to reach a compromise agreement on the transition to a new administration. The Ayatollah, however, persistently refused to receive anyone who had "co-operated" with the Bakhtiar regime. During a visit to France on Jan.22, Mr Tehrani resigned as chairman of the Regency Council, echoing the Ayatollah's line that it was an "illegal" body.

Anti-government protests continued after the Shah's flight and intensified following the announcement by Khomeini on Jan.20 that he would return to the country on Jan.26. Troops opened fire on demonstrators in Ahwaz and Dezful on Jan.17–18, although other major rallies passed off peacefully after Khomeini had appealed to his followers to avoid clashes with security forces lest the army use them as a pretext for staging a military coup. (Several reports at this time indicated that royalist officers were preparing for just such a move.) Evidence of continuing support for the Bakhtiar government included a major demonstration on Jan.25, when some 100,000 people marched peacefully through Tehran, claiming to represent the "silent majority" of pro-government Iranians. On the same day, the government reimposed a ban on marches and demonstrations in all towns and cities under martial law. This effort to re-establish control of the streets failed completely to stem the growing wave of protest.

Bakhtiar continued to hope for a compromise with Khomeini, however. On Jan.24, he presented a "final offer" to the Ayatollah, in which he offered to resign on condition that Khomeini disbanded the "provisional government", delayed his return for three weeks to allow the Prime Minister "to please and quieten the Army", and supported the holding of elections for a constituent assembly, which would decide whether Iran should be a monarchy or an Islamic republic. Bakhtiar also suggested a merger of the Regency and Revolutionary Councils or the allocation of equal veto power to both bodies. The following day Khomeini did agree to delay his return, but stressed that this did not indicate a willingness to co-operate with the government. (In practice, Khomeini's immediate return was prevented by the closure of Tehran and other major airports by army units.) Rumours that Khomeini had agreed to talks with Bakhtiar in Paris were confounded on Jan.29 when the Ayatollah repeated his insistence that the government was illegal and that he would not meet Bakhtiar until the latter had resigned as Prime Minister. While Bakhtiar rejected this demand as "unacceptable", the government later announced that Khomeini was free to return.

Meanwhile anti-government protests continued. On Jan.26 troops opened fire on crowds in Tehran who, unaware of the airport's closure, had congregated in the city to welcome Khomeini. Over 100 people were reported to have been killed. Numerous other violent clashes took place during late January, with soldiers frequently resorting to firearms and opposition leaders encouraging their supporters to attack police and army units. On Jan.28, troops clashed with rioters in Tehran's Isfahan Square following a demonstration in which crowds chanted "Death to Bakhtiar!". Three days later thousands of troops, many shouting "Long Live the Shah!", drove through the streets of Tehran in a show of strength to demonstrate their willingness to fight for the government.

On Feb.1, 1979 Ayatollah Khomeini returned to Iran, receiving a tumultuous welcome at Tehran's airport, where an estimated 3,000,000 people turned out to greet him. Martial law regulations had been lifted in Tehran for the occasion. From the airport Khomeini travelled to the capital's main Behest Zahran cemetery, where many of the victims of the past years' disturbances had been buried. Thousands of supporters lined the route of his motorcade and the last part of the journey had to be undertaken by helicopter as the massive crowds made progress by road impossible. At the cemetery, Khomeini made a brief speech in which he reiterated his contention that the present government and parliament were illegal, and warned that he would "shut the mouths" of Bakhtiar and his government if they refused to resign. He appealed to the armed forces not to be "left out of step with history" and to join forces with the Islamic movement. The following day, Khomeini rejected an offer by Bakhtiar to form a coalition government, and called on his followers to step up their efforts to bring down the government, principally through industrial action, which continued to effectively paralyse many sectors of the economy.

At a press conference on Feb.2, Khomeini promised the rapid establishment of a provisional government, assured minority groups and foreigners that they would be well treated under the Islamic regime (with the exception of "those who have taken sides against us") and insisted that unless Bakhtiar resigned, he would institute a *jihad* (holy war) against the government. In reply, Bakhtiar asserted that a *jihad* could not be "declared against other Moslems. You can never turn a Moslem against a Moslem. That is a threat of fratricide. But if they are armed, we will answer a bullet with a bullet". Two days later, the Prime Minister threatened to arrest and execute anyone calling for the overthrow of the government by force.

On Feb.5, Ayatollah Khomeini announced that Dr Mehdi Bazargan had been appointed Prime Minister of a provisional government. He warned that anyone who acted against this government would be violating "sacred religious laws" and would be severely punished. For his part, Bazargan said that he would shortly announce a "shadow cabinet", and that in the meantime he was preparing for a forceful response from the army.

Bazargan, then aged 73, had studied in France for six years and served in the Mossadeq government in the early 1950s. After the overthrow of the Mossadeq regime, he founded the National Resistance Movement (which joined the National Front in 1962), and in 1977 helped form the Iranian Committee for the Defence of Liberty and Human Rights. He had been imprisoned on four occasions. Widely considered as a moderate, Bazargan had maintained close ties with both the secular and religious oppositions to the Shah.

Appealing to Bakhtiar to resign and hand over power to him, Bazargan set out his programme on Feb.9 for a referendum on the Islamic Republic question, the appointment of a constituent assembly and eventual parliamentary elections. The two rival premiers had several meetings in an effort to find a compromise arrangement, but publicly Bakhtiar remained defiant. Addressing the *Majlis* on Feb.5, he asserted that "Iran is one country, one government and one constitution . . . if anyone goes ahead and forms a new government, I shall tolerate it only as a joke".

Control over the country was rapidly slipping from Bakhtiar's grasp, however. Rallies of Khomeini's supporters in Tehran streets on Feb.7–8 included uniformed soldiers, clasping flowers as a symbol of peaceful opposition. In some cities, notably Isfahan, Shiraz and Qom, followers of the Ayatollah had taken virtual control of public services and local courts by Feb.7. In the holy city of Qom in particular (overseen by Ayatollah Shariatmadari), martial law regulations were no longer observed and the regular police force had been replaced by 500 unarmed "Islamic guards". While strikes continued on Khomeini's orders in other towns and cities, a "Khomeini welcome committee" was set up in Qom to run a chain of co-operative shops to ensure the continued supply of food and other essential goods. An "Islamic tax" of one-fifth of each family's annual savings replaced the government system. A few pro-Shah demonstrations took place, and a "National Unity Front" was formed to support the Bakhtiar government, but overall during the first ten days of February, the tide of popular support for Ayatollah Khomeini continued to rise.

FALL OF BAKHTIAR GOVERNMENT AND ASSUMPTION OF POWER BY THE ISLAMIC REVOLUTION

The Bakhtiar government fell on Feb.11 following two days of fierce fighting in Tehran between troops loyal to the government on one hand, and supporters of Ayatollah Khomeini aided by dissident members of the air force on the other; an estimated 200–300 people were killed in Tehran alone. Fighting had broken out on Feb.9 when troops from the elite Imperial Guard had attacked a display of support for Khomeini staged by a group of airforce technicians at the Doshan Tappeh air base. Over the next two days, anti-government forces seized control of a number of military garrisons. Power was finally surrendered to Ayatollah Khomeini's movement on Feb.11 after the army command had ordered all soldiers to return to barracks and Gen. Qharabaghi had assured Dr Bazargan of his support for the provisional government. Bakhtiar formally resigned on the evening of Feb.11 following a meeting with Bazargan. He subsequently went into exile abroad.

Sporadic fighting continued over the next few days, and there were clashes between the *Mujaheddin-e Khalq* and the far left *Cherik Fedayeen-e Khalq*. Armed groups attacked foreigners and ransacked the US embassy. Order was eventually restored on Feb.15.

Bazargan's cabinet, as announced on Feb.12–13, included two well-known National Front leaders, Mr Dariush Foruhar (Labour and Social Affairs) and Dr Karim Sanjabi (Foreign Affairs) and close aides of the Ayatollah, as well as a number of technocrats.

The new regime achieved a degree of constitutional legitimacy as a result of a referendum held on March 30–31, 1979, in which voters were asked, "Are you for the replacement of the monarchy by an Islamic Republic, the constitution of which will be approved — yes or no?" Official results showed that of the 20,288,021 persons taking part, all but 140,966 (all of them in Tehran) voted "yes". Considerable controversy resulted from the fact that the ballot was not secret; voters had to produce identity documents and indicate their preference by detaching part of the ballot paper.

Parties supporting the "yes" vote included Sanjabi and Foruhar's National Front, the Moslem People's Republican Party (MPRP) — composed of the followers of the "moderate" Ayatollah Shariatmadari — and the Tudeh

Party. Both the *Mujaheddin* and *Fedayeen-e Khalq* movements criticized the wording of the referendum as offering electors little real choice. The principal Kurdish groups called for a boycott, as did the recently-formed National Democratic Front. Its leader, Mr Matine-Daftari (grandson of the late Dr Mossadeq), asserted that it was "anti-democratic to expect people to choose between a government which they had themselves overthrown and a system of government as yet unknown".

A draft constitution published on June 18 contained provisions for a nationally-elected president and a unicameral parliament. It promised an independent judiciary, full human rights and religious tolerance towards Zoroastrians, Jews and Christians (but with no specific mention of Bahais). A Council of Guardians, composed of clerics, judges and law professors, would ensure that "no laws can be passed in contradiction with Islam".

Elections were held on Aug.3 to a 73-member Constituent Council of Experts, which would finalize the constitution. Over 80 per cent of the 1,000 candidates were fundamentalist clerics. In addition to the newly-formed Islamic Republic Party, the elections were contested by the *Mujaheddin* and *Fedayeen* movements and the Tudeh Party. The National Front, National Democratic Front and MPRP called for a boycott on the grounds that there could be no free elections in the current atmosphere of civil disturbance. The National Front in particular complained of restrictions on its attempts to campaign. Those elected included the *Mujaheddin* leader, Massoud Rajavi, and Abolhassan Bani-Sadr. Representatives of the Zoroastrian, Jewish and Christian candidates were guaranteed a seat.

The principal amendments made by the Council enshrined the Shia branch of Islam as the country's official religion, and gave supreme power to the pre-eminent Shia religious leader—the *Wali Faqi*—who was to be chosen on the basis of ideas developed by Khomeini in his book, *Wilayat e-Faqi* ("Rule of the Theologian"). In the event of there being no generally recognized spiritual authority (as currently represented by Khomeini himself), the theologian's rule was to be exercised by a college of clerics.

The Constitution was approved by referendum on Dec.2–3, 1979 when an estimated 65 per cent turnout of the electorate approved it by 15,680,329 votes to 78,516. Doubts were cast on the validity of the ballot since it was again not held in secret. It was widely boycotted in the national minority regions of Kurdistan, Baluchistan and Azerbaijan. Among those supporting a boycott were Ayatollah Shariatmadari, whose stand resulted in his being placed under virtual house arrest at his home in Qom.

While the new regime successfully foiled coup plans by pro-Shah elements, its authority was split between the Bazargain government in Tehran and

B

Ayatollah Khomeini's Revolutionary Council in Qom. The government repeatedly complained that its powers were severely limited, partly as a result of subservience to the Revolutionary Council, and partly due to powers assumed by other bodies. Notable among these were the Revolutionary Courts, headed by the fundamentalist Islamic judge, Ayatollah Sadeq Khalkali, the *Komitehs*, or revolutionary committees, set up in the main by left-leaning clerics or political groups, and the Revolutionary Guards, or *Pasdaran*.

The Revolutionary Guards had been formed on Khomeini's orders in March 1979 to combine the functions of an army, a police force and the mosque, and to have the power "to spread Iran's Islamic revolution throughout the world". Directly responsible to the Revolutionary Council, the Guards by May 1979 had over 10,000 permanent members and some 100,000 "reservists".

Provincial governors appointed by the government were often ineffectual because of disagreements between members of the civil administration, the local clergy responsible to a Khomeini nominee and disparate armed revolutionary committees.

Bazargan complained on May 23 that Iran had become "a nation of hundreds of chiefs", adding that "the decision-making roles in our country are so numerous that they have paralysed much activity; it would be impossible for any President of the country to work under these circumstances". Among ministers resigning from the provisional government in its early months were Dr Sanjabi, who complained of "disorders created by a government within a government".

On July 19, however, Bazargan announced that agreement had been reached with Khomeini on the sharing of power between the government and the Revolutionary Council by which a number of leading council members would be appointed to the government as Deputy Ministers. However, by early November, the persisting tensions between the government and the Council left Bazargan unable to continue. He presented his resignation to Khomeini on Nov.5. The following day, the Ayatollah announced that the Revolutionary Council would take over the running of the country while preparing for elections for a consultative assembly and a national President.

Abolhassan Bani-Sadr was elected as the Islamic Republic's first President on Jan.25, 1980, beating his seven rivals by a comfortable margin, and gaining 75 per cent of the total votes cast. He was subsequently appointed head of the Revolutionary Council and commander-in-chief. Over 100 people had sought the nomination, but only eight were allowed to stand. Among those disqualified were Mehdi Bazargan and Massoud Rajavi. Second place (with 2.24 million votes to Bani-Sadr's 10.75 million) went to Rear-Admiral Ahmad Madani, who was mainly supported by the educated and westernized middle class. Despite issuing statements replete with revolutionary fervour, Bani-Sadr was widely seen as a moderate, and was soon to come into conflict with the radicals over the US hostage issue (see pp. 53–56).

TIGHTENING OF ISLAMIC CONTROL

Faced with the persisting threat of a pro-Shah coup, the new regime's special revolutionary courts carried out summary trials and executions of over 600 officials of the former regime. The most prominent of these was Dr Amir Abbas Hoveida, Prime Minister under the Shah from 1965–77, who was executed on April 7. The executions continued in the face of severe misgivings expressed by a number of leading politicians. Dr Bazargan on March 14 described them as "a disgrace" which detracted from "the glory of our revolution". They were also condemned by the International Commission of Jurists. In an effort to regularize the situation, Ayatollah Khomeini on April 14 instructed revolutionary prosecutors to ask for the death penalty only for people guilty of murder or torture. From July 10, onwards, it was forbidden to make any arrest without warrant from the Prosecutor-General. Three months later, acting on orders from Ayatollah Khomeini, the Prosecutor-General ordered all Islamic courts to suspend executions.

Despite these moves, reports emerged of continued executions, detentions without trial and even torture of detainees. Reports in the Western press in early August 1980 suggested that since the revolution more than 1,250 people had been executed. The victims included military personnel suspected of plotting against the regime, left-wing opposition activists, drug traffickers and sexual offenders. Women, Bahais and Jews were among those executed. Over 300 people were detained following an attempted coup by air force officers in June 1980 to return Shapour Bakhtiar to power. Among the 100 or so executed in connection with it was Gen. Sayed Mehdeyoun, who had served briefly as Air Force Commander after the revolution. SAVAK was replaced in August 1979 by the "Iranian National Information and Security Organization", to operate both inside and outside the country.

Within weeks of the revolution, the alliance between the secular and religious movements which had joined together to overthrow the Shah began to crack. Khomeini and his aides denounced Marxism and atheism. After a number of demonstrations organized by leftist and liberal groups, up to 500,000 people gathered in Tehran on July 17 in response to an appeal by Khomeini, shouting slogans denouncing the Left as "agents of SAVAK". Over the ensuing months, the split between Islam and the Left was to become unbridgeable.

New press laws announced in August provided for prison sentences for publication of defamatory or untruthful reports about Ayatollah Khomeini, the Prime Minister or future heads of state, while persons connected with the Shah's regime were forbidden from contributing to the press. Demonstrations against press censorship provoked clashes between fundamentalist activists and National Front supporters; the government denounced the protest as a "counter-revolutionary plot", and demonstrations without prior permission were banned on Aug.14. A week later, Khomeini ordered the closure of 22 newspapers and magazines, including those of the National Front, *Fedayeen* and also the Tudeh Party, whose offices were closed by revolutionary guards. The country's two leading dailies, *Kayhan* and *Ettelaat*, were nationalized on Sept.9 on the grounds that they were "pillars of the former regime" and had "profited from foreign capital".

Within weeks of the revolution, Islamic (*Sharia*) law was being applied across wide areas of Iranian society. In particular, marriage legislation was amended to conform with the prescriptions of the Koran, and strong pressure was applied to encourage women to adopt the chador (full-length black veil). This in turn led to protest demonstrations by several thousand women in Tehran. Birth control within marriage was permitted to continue, however. A ban was placed on imports of frozen meat, luxury goods and alcoholic beverages. On July 23, Khomeini called for a ban on all music on Iranian radio on the grounds that music made the brain "inactive and frivolous", and was "a betrayal of the nation's youth". In June 1980, the Ministry of Arts announced the closure of all the country's cinemas.

Iran's economy had taken a battering from the months of strikes and industrial unrest in the run-up to the revolution. The situation improved following the resumption on March 5 of oil exports, which had been practically suspended since December 1978. Large numbers of major contracts with Western companies were cancelled or suspended, and on March 20 all foreign workers ordered to leave the country unless their work was essential to Iran's economy. A month later, the government stated that the number of foreigners in Iran had been reduced to around 10,000 from 250,000 under the Shah. The country's banks, insurance companies and almost all large- and medium-sized industrial enterprises were nationalized, on Khomeini's orders, during June and July. A year after the revolution, the economy had been reorganized along broadly Islamic lines, although the extent of state intervention was to remain a controversial issue for many years to come.

Rafsanjani holds court (*K. Golestan—Reflex*)

Ready for martyrdom—the Revolutionary Guards (*Nick Danziger*)

THE ISLAMIC REPUBLIC

SUPPRESSION OF INTERNAL OPPOSITION—ALIENATION OF MINORITIES

In mid-1980, with the new Republic apparently secure from immediate overthrow, Ayatollah Khomeini felt able to launch an "Islamic cultural revolution", urging widespread purges to rid Iran of "counter-revolutionaries" and all vestiges of the Shah's regime. Speaking on June 27, he criticized the government, revolutionary council and President Bani-Sadr for failing to establish a "truly Islamic country", and instituted large-scale dismissals of government employees, particularly in the state oil company, the Foreign Ministry and the education sector. There was also a major shake-up among senior officers in the armed forces and even the revolutionary guard. Opposition activists overseas became the target of assassination attempts: in two incidents in July 1980, Dr Bakhtiar survived an attempt on his life in his Paris flat, while Ali Tabatabai, a former diplomat at the Iranian embassy in the USA and leader of the anti-Khomeini "Freedom Foundation", was shot dead in Washington. Over the ensuing years, exiled opponents of the regime were targets of a number of attacks and assassinations.

Iran's Kurdish, Arab and Baluchi minorities initially supported the revolution in the light of Khomeini's undertakings that they would be well-treated. During 1979–80, however, the regime's failure to meet their hopes for autonomy, coupled with its imposition of strict Shia Islamic law, alienated much of this early support. In December 1979, responding in particular to Kurdish unrest, the government outlined a plan by which certain regions could be designated "self-governing", enjoying local economic autonomy. In general, however, the leadership feared that major concessions towards autonomous demands could seriously jeopardize the unity of Iran, and that some groups wanted complete separatism rather than a degree of self-rule under the Islamic regime.

Fighting between Kurdish guerrillas and government troops broke out in Sanandaj, the provincial capital, in March 1979. A full-scale government offensive succeeded in bringing the main Kurdish towns under control by September 1979, although sporadic battles continued over the ensuing months between Kurdish Democratic Party and Komaleh guerrillas on the one hand and government troops and revolutionary guards on the other, despite the government's offer of regional autonomy. The Kurdish insurgency remained a thorn in the side of the Islamic Republic throughout its first decade. Kurdish guerrillas continued to control large areas of the countryside in the face of repeated government assaults. In the early years of the Gulf War, they received some assistance from Iraq, although this was curtailed by Iranian victories in the border area.

Unrest among the 2,000,000 Arabs in the oil-rich Khuzistan province erupted in May 1979, after a period of mounting tension as Arab representatives demanded local autonomy, a greater share of oil revenues and an end to alleged job discrimination in favour of the province's minority Persian community. Fighting between armed Arabs and local revolutionary guards intensified after the breakdown of negotiations, and in July militant Arabs embarked on a campaign of sabotage attacks, particularly targeted at the oil industry. Evidence of Iraqi assistance to the rebels heightened the tension between the two countries in the run-up to the Iraqi invasion of Iran. In April 1980, the Iranian embassy in London was seized by armed militants calling themselves the "Group of the Martyr", who demanded the release of 91 fellow Arabs imprisoned in Khuzistan. After two hostages had been shot dead, the embassy was stormed by British SAS commandos, who freed the remaining hostages and killed five of the six gunmen. Arab resistance largely disappeared in the wake of the Iraqi invasion, with most Iranian Arabs rallying to Iran's defence.

In addition, members of Iran's Bahai community, a Moslem sect regarded as heretical by mainstream Islam, also faced discrimination and maltreatment as thousands were dismissed from their jobs and had their property confiscated. Bahai shrines were desecrated, and some leading Bahais were arrested and executed. The free movement of Jews was curtailed and some wishing to emigrate to Israel were prevented from doing so on the grounds that this was "a Zionist act". Some were also reported to have been executed.

FALL OF BANI-SADR AND THE MUJAHEDDIN'S ARMED STRUGGLE, 1980–82

President Bani-Sadr was formally sworn into office in July 1980 by the newly-elected *Majlis*. The elections had represented a significant setback for the President, with the hard-line fundamentalist Islamic Republican Party (IRP) and its supporters winning over half the 245 seats, compared to 74 claimed by Bani-Sadr's supporters. Allegations of vote-rigging and interference were levelled at the Islamic leadership by both the Tudeh Party and the *Mujaheddin*, which was increasingly attracting the support of the educated classes and the moderate left. The new Prime Minister was Mohammed Ali Radjai, an IRP supporter who had been involved in revolutionary politics since the early 1960s.

Bani-Sadr quickly came into conflict with Radjai over the latter's choice of Cabinet, which was dominated by fundamentalists. The President eventually gave in to pressure from Ayatollah Khomeini and the *Majlis* to accept most of Radjai's proposed appointments. However, he was soon to find himself at loggerheads with the rest of the government. Bani-Sadr expressed reservations over the occupation of the US embassy by militant students in November 1979, and worked for a rapid settlement by which the hostages could be freed in return for limited concessions from the USA. Across a range of issues, the President favoured a more moderate approach than the Islamic radicals, whom he accused of subverting his authority. Increasingly, he came to depend on the support of the *Mujaheddin*, while the fundamentalist line was taken to the streets by the *Hezbollah* (Party of God).

Matters came to a head when over 500 *Hezbollahi* disrupted a speech by Bani-Sadr at Tehran University on March 5, 1981. The President called on his supporters to turn on the hecklers, over 40 of whom were injured in the ensuing melee. Identity cards and documents taken from them revealed that they were closely associated with the revolutionary leadership. Leading clerics demanded that Bani-Sadr be brought to trial for inciting the trouble, while the President complained that his "enemies had planned the violence" and called on the Iranian public to "smash attempts at establishing the rule of violence rather than the rule of law". While Ayatollah Khomeini initially urged reconciliation between the two sides, tension between them increased when the IRP-dominated *Majlis* passed bills in May which would have secured control over all senior appointments for the Cabinet, thereby by-passing the President. Bani-Sadr refused to sign the bills into law, leading Khomeini to implicitly condemn him by warning that anyone who defied the *Majlis* would be "pursued as a corrupt person on earth" (a crime punishable by death under Islamic law). An arbitration committee set up after the March disturbance declared that the President had violated the constitution by refusing to sign the *Majlis* bills. From now on, Bani-Sadr's downfall was swift. Newspapers sympathetic to the President were closed down and leading supporters arrested. He was relieved of the post of Commander-in-Chief on June 10, and, against a background of street-fighting between his supporters and radicals, the *Majlis* declared him politically incompetent. On June 22, he was dismissed by Ayatollah Khomeini. Five weeks later, he fled into exile in France accompanied by the *Mujaheddin* leader, Massoud Rajavi.

The following month, Radjai was elected President by an overwhelming majority. Bani-Sadr joined opposition groups in calling for a boycott, and there were allegations that people were coerced into voting by threats of subsequent harrassment. The elections were marked by numerous opposition attacks on government targets.

In the wake of Bani-Sadr's ousting, the regime launched a vigorous campaign to eradicate all opposition, particularly that of the *Mujaheddin*. Numerous arrests and executions were met with a campaign of bombing and assassinations. In one of the more spectacular attacks, 74 leading politicians, including Ayatollah Behesti, chairman of the IRP, and four cabinet ministers, were killed on June 28, 1981, when a bomb devastated the Tehran headquarters of the IRP. Although not claimed by them, the incident was widely attributed to the *Mujaheddin*. In response, the authorities arrested and executed over 200 of the group's members and sympathizers. Despite government efforts, opposition attacks continued by both the *Mujaheddin* and the left-wing *Fedayeen e-Khalq*, with pitched battles taking place between the rebels and revolutionary guards units in Tehran and elsewhere. Although the majority of the population, together with the armed forces, remained neutral in the conflict, the *Mujaheddin* were understood to enjoy widespread support in Kurdistan and other ethnic minority areas. Alarmed at the quickening cycle of violence, more than 70 *Majlis* MPs warned Khomeini in early August that they would resign unless the unrest was ended by political means.

The *Mujaheddin* struck a devasting blow on Aug.30 when an incendiary device exploded during a top-level meeting at the Prime Minister's office, killing President Radjai, the new Prime Minister, Hojatolislam Bahonar, and the Chief of Police. The device had been planted by a senior security official who turned out to have been a member of the *Mujaheddin*. Ironically, the meeting had been called to discuss the *Mujaheddin* threat. Attacks continued through September; the revolutionary prosecutor-general, Hojatolislam Ghodoussi, was killed by a bomb planted in his office on Sept.5. Six days later, Ayatollah Madani, a close aide of Khomeini, was killed in Tabriz when a "suicide bomber" detonated a hand grenade while standing next to him at Friday prayers. By the end of the month, *Mujaheddin* fighters were engaging revolutionary guards in the streets of central Tehran using machine-guns and rocket-propelled grenades. Limited armed action was also undertaken by monarchist supporters.

The regime responded to the challenge by rounding up and executing hundreds of *Mujaheddin* sympathizers; estimates of the total number of political prisoners held in mid-1982 varied between 30,000 and 50,000, while Amnesty International reported that over 2,500 executions had taken place in the eight months since June 1981. During 1982, there were reports of detainees being executed for crimes with which they had no connection, as the authorities would react to an incident such as a bomb explosion or an attack on revolutionary guards by executing a number of people already detained on various charges. Numerous reports of torture were given wide publicity by exile sources. An Iranian spokesman rejected expressions of concern by the UN Committee on Human Rights, declaring that "our people have decided to remain free and independent and Islamic and not be fooled by the imperialist myth of human rights". The former Prime Minister, Mehdi Bazargan, was sharply criticized for speaking out against the executions and the "atmosphere of violence" in Iran. Nevertheless, he appealed to Khomeini to "stop and rethink before it is too late".

The wave of repression had its effect, however. Although *Mujaheddin* and other opposition groups continued their attacks through 1982–83, the threat which they posed to the regime gradually diminished, and by the end of 1984 their activities were by and large reduced to sporadic assassinations and bomb attacks, with many of their original leaders either killed or in exile. As with the anti-Shah opposition, the majority of the exiled opponents of Khomeini came to be based in Paris. Despite exhortations by the French government to refrain from political activity, Bani-Sadr and Rajavi announced the formation of the "National Resistance Council for Liberty and Independence", and conducted a propaganda war against the Iranian regime.

Meanwhile, on April 11, 1982 the Tehran authorities announced that they had uncovered a plot to kill Ayatollah Khomeini and seize power. The former Foreign Minister, Sadeq Qotbzadeh, was among 44 people arrested in connection with the plan, which was reported to have had the blessing of Ayatollah Shariatmadari. Qotbzadeh was executed in September after a trial at which he had admitted to charges of trying to overthrow the Islamic Republic. Other executions followed. Qotbzadeh's relative moderation as Foreign Minister (when he had opposed putting the US embassy hostages on trial) had earned him the opposition of the radicals in the regime, who by the end of 1981 were firmly in control.

The October 1981 presidential elections were won by Hojatolislam Ali Khamenei—the first cleric to hold the post. Khamenei, then aged 42, had received military training in Palestinian camps in Lebanon, and had taken part in the street fighting on the eve of the Shah's flight. He enjoyed considerable authority in his twin roles as Khomeini's personal representative on the Supreme Defence Council and secretary-general of the IRP. The new Prime Minister was Hossein Moussavi, aged 39, a co-founder of the IRP and Foreign Minister since July 1981, who was widely regarded as a hard-line fundamentalist.

ISLAMIZATION AND REFORM, 1982–85

With the opposition in retreat, Khomeini announced on Aug.22, 1982, that all laws passed under the Shah which were not in line with the tenets of Islam would be annulled. The Supreme Court advised magistrates to base their judgments on "religious texts or authentic sermons", and, if in doubt, to consult religious leaders. The consumption of alcohol and practice of homosexuality were both made punishable by death, while couples found kissing in public would receive 100 lashes. Students were enjoined to "watch the behaviour of their teachers and report deviants to the authorities". There were also reports of people being stoned to death for committing adultery, while women who went about unveiled were subjected to harrassment.

The radicals received something of a setback in May when the Council of Guardians ruled that a *Majlis* bill to nationalize foreign trade was contrary to Islamic principles, despite the fact that it had been strongly supported by Ayatollah Khomeini. Radical factions were also disappointed by the leadership's failure to designate Ayatollah Hossein Ali Montazeri, Khomeini's son-in-law, as his successor. Instead, elections were held in October 1982 to an "Assembly of Experts", which would have the task of choosing the next *wali faqi*.

By the end of 1982, the leadership was taking steps to win back public confidence. Rafsanjani admitted in December that "counter-revolutionaries" had "to some extent been sucessful in brutalizing the government". Declaring that "the people should feel their lives and dignity secure", Khomeini called a halt to "un-Islamic practices" such as torture, detention without a court order, mail interception and phone-tapping. The Chief of Police and Prosecutor-General were replaced, and investigation teams were set up to look into alleged human rights abuses across the country. The notorious Tehran revolutionary prosecutor, Assadollah Lajverdi, was sacked in mid-1985, along with a number of officials at the capital's Evin jail, where many of the country's political prisoners were incarcerated. Despite these gestures, opposition groups and international human rights organizations continued to report cases of torture throughout the mid-1980s, although by this stage there was evidence that the regime was becoming more sensitive to world opinion. Meanwhile, emissaries were despatched early in 1983 to entice exiles to return home with promises of safe treatment. The Council of Guardians had earlier ruled unconstitutional a *Majlis* bill providing for confiscation of exiles'property. The moves represented an effort by the regime to stem the flow of defections of badly-needed skilled workers, scientists and businessmen.

During 1983, limited toleration was also accorded to the moderate opposition, epitomized by Mehdi Bazargan's "Freedom Movement", which, among other things, advocated a peaceful settlement of the Gulf War. In rare overt protests against the regime, several thousand Tehran residents responded to calls by opposition radios to mark the August anniversary of the 1907 constitution by staging "traffic-jam" demonstrations, forming their cars into queues around middle-class districts of the capital. Women flouted Islamic dress strictures by appearing unveiled and wearing light make-up. The *Majlis* meanwhile had approved a bill which reintroduced the right of women to institute divorce proceedings, so long as they had "moral or ideological" grounds for doing so. In September 1984, Hojatolislam Rafsanjani, Speaker of the *Majlis* and an increasingly influential figure, condemned "political extremists" who demanded absolute segregation between the sexes and opposed women having any role in public life. In the same speech, Rafsanjani criticized aspects of the "personality cult" surrounding Khomeini, particularly the all-pervasive display of the Ayatollah's picture.

The Tudeh was less privileged, however. Aware of its potential threat as a focus of opposition as it grew progressively distanced from the regime, the government moved decisively during 1983 to crush the Party once and for all. It was declared illegal in May, and most of its leaders were arrested. In televised "confessions" over the ensuing months, leading members admitted to carrying out spying for Moscow and other treasonable offences. Among those detained and subsequently executed for these offences was the commander of Iran's navy, Capt. Bahram Afzali. Tehran's uncertainty over the loyalty of its armed forces was borne out in May 1983, when security forces foiled a plan by air force officers to bomb Khomeini's residence.

Elections to the second "Islamic Consultative Assembly" (*Majlis*) in April 1984 produced a clear victory for "progressive" elements, favoured by Khomeini, over a "conservative" alliance of provincial clerics and *bazaaris* (merchants). Bazargan's Freedom Movement, which had five supporters in the previous *Majlis*, boycotted the elections in protest at government restrictions on their freedom to campaign. Far from being a rubber stamp of approval for the leadership's wishes, the *Majlis* was frequently the scene of heated debates, in which the government regularly came under fire and ministers were forced into resignation through the passage of votes of no-confidence.

The radicals became further entrenched through the re-election in August 1985 of President Khamenei, who defeated his nearest rival, Mahmoud Kashani, (another radical) by over 12,000,000 votes to 1,500,000. A conservative candidate supported by the *bazaari* faction scored less than 300,000 votes. However, blank votes cast as a protest against the regime numbered over 350,000, and there was some evidence that many electors had responded to calls by opposition groups to boycott the poll, with almost half of the registered electorate failing to turn out. Bazargan's application to stand had been rejected by the Council of Guardians, although a number of leading government figures, including Moussavi, had apparently favoured his candidacy as a means of demonstrating the extent of political freedom under the regime.

THE EMERGING POWER STRUGGLE, 1986–88

Internal divisions within the Iranian leadership became increasingly apparent during the mid–late 1980s. Moussavi's reappointment as Prime Minister in October 1985 took place against the wishes of President Khamenei, who favoured the appointment of a cabinet including conservative business leaders with a more moderate figure at its head. Moussavi secured the premiership only after the intervention of Ayatollah Khomeini himself; even then the *Majlis's* vote of confidence in him was passed by only 162 votes in favour to 73 against (with 26 abstentions)—itself evidence of the extent of the disagreement. This issue had been the subject of relatively open press debate, with the IRP's newspaper, *Islamic Republic*, calling on the leadership "to resist attempts to appoint a coalition government including representatives of the propertied class".

A month later, the Assembly of Experts announced that Ayatollah Montazeri, generally viewed as having radical sympathies, had been designated as successor to Khomeini. The decision was not widely publicized within Iran, however, and Montazeri himself later announced that he saw it as "a *fait accompli*", which went "against the wishes of my heart", and that he intended to ask the Assembly to withdraw the designation. While this was never accomplished, Montazeri failed to take a dominant position in Iranian politics. Instead, the pivotal role was being assumed increasingly by Hashemi Rafsanjani, the *Majlis* Speaker.

Another point of issue between "radical" and "conservative" (or "pragmatic") politicians was the role of private enterprise. This was brought into focus by the decline of Iran's economic fortunes, which, in common with most other petroleum exporting countries, had been badly affected by the falling oil prices and revenues. In Iran's case, the oil revenue problem had been exacerbated by production and sales losses due to Iraqi air attacks. High levels of military expenditure necessitated by the war also put the economy under strain. After three years of growth averaging 25 per cent annually, there was zero growth in 1985, while corruption among state employees was reaching endemic levels: the Interior Minister admitted in late 1985 that this problem was causing the government more worry than the war with Iraq.

Against this background, Ayatollah Khomeini made several interventions encouraging private investment, warning the government "not to nationalize everything" and emphasizing the importance of people taking an active role in the country's affairs, particularly by engaging in business and trade. Remarks such as these helped prevent the powerful *bazaari* class from becoming wholly alienated from the regime. Rafsanjani drew attention to the divisions among the leadership on the issue, when he referred in June 1986 to "two distinct ideological frameworks, one favouring state control, the other not". The debate was also played out by newspapers supporting rival viewpoints.

During 1987, the "pragmatists" grouped around Rafsanjani extended their influence over the regime, while the aging Ayatollah Khomeini played a diminishing role in Iranian politics. Their growing authority was epitomized by the execution in September of Mehdi Hashemi, an associate of Montazeri. Hashemi ran the "World Islamic Organization", whose aims of exporting the Islamic revolution had run counter to Rafsanjani's attempts to put Iran's relations with other countries on a more even footing. More seriously, Hashemi was also suspected of leaking to the Beirut press details of the clandestine contacts underway between Iranian leaders and the USA in the "arms-for-hostages" affair (see pp. 56–57), in which Rafsanjani was deeply implicated. After failing to intercede on Hashemi's behalf, Montazeri's influence began to decline. His office was placed under the control of Khomeini's son, Ahmad, (who was by now effectively controlling access to his father) and Ayatollah Meshkini (brother-in-law of Hojatolislam Reyshahri, the Information Minister, who was in turn a close ally of Rafsanjani). Montazeri's position as heir-apparent was further weakened in December when Khomeini presented a revized version of his political testament to the Iranian leadership. Although its contents were not disclosed, it reportedly stated that the leadership would not be passed to a single theologian as previously set down, but to an elected three- or five-man council. Khomeini himself announced the disbandment of the IRP in June 1987, commenting that instead of being a "united forum for encountering prevailing problems" it had become instead "an excuse for discord and factionalism".

These changes took place against a background of unprecedented public criticisms of the conduct of the war with Iraq. Several hundred revolutionary guards staged a demonstration in central Tehran in May calling for an end to the war on the basis of forgiveness of the Iraqi President, Saddam Hussein. Among leaflets demanding an end to the fighting which were circulating in the capital during Summer 1987 was one signed by Gen. Azizollah Rahimi, a former military commander under the Shah who had initially supported the Islamic regime. Rahimi was linked with the newly-established Association for Defence of the Freedom and Sovereignty of the Iranian Nation, formed by Dr Bazargan and seven members of his 1979 provisional government. The government's toleration of the Association's activities was resented by the radicals. Several members of the Association were arrested in May 1988 after it circulated an open letter denouncing the leadership's conduct of the war and other "erroneous policies". There was also criticism of the war during 1988 by leading conservative clerics, while unconfirmed reports spoke of violent anti-Khomeini protests in Isfahan and elsewhere.

Meanwhile the exiled opposition was itself becoming divided. Ex-President Bani-Sadr and *Mujaheddin* leader Massoud Rajavi fell out over the latter's decision to ally with Saddam Hussein. From June 1986 onwards, the *Mujaheddin* were based in Iraq, where they benefited from logistical support and training and were able to launch a number of cross-border raids in the guise of the "National Liberation Army". This overt alliance with the enemy cost them some support at home, however. For its part, after the death of the Shah in 1980, monarchist opposition to the regime became increasingly irrelevant.

Elections to the third *Majlis* in April–May 1988 produced a majority for "reformist" groups—who supported Moussavi's policies of greater state control over the economy through nationalization and land reform—over candidates favoured by the *bazaari* class and provincial religious leaders, who advocated a more conservative economic policy favouring private business. The new balance of power in the parliament was demonstrated by its approval of Moussavi as Prime Minister by an overwhelming 204 votes to eight, with five abstentions. Earlier, in January, Khomeini had established a special assembly, or "Expediency Council", of six senior clerics and seven leading government officials which would have the power to decide issues by majority vote whenever the *Majlis* and the Council of Guardians were unable to agree. In doing so, Khomeini was attempting to prevent further ideological deadlock between the two bodies; the conservative Council of Guardians had blocked the passage of reformist legislation on foreign trade and the ownership of agricultural land and industries, on the grounds that it ran counter to Islam's respect for private property.

Rafsanjani's position at the centre of Iranian politics was strengthened in June 1988 when Khomeini appointed him acting Commander-in-Chief of the armed forces (Khomeini himself being the formal Commander-in-Chief, according to the constitution). Rafsanjani was already chief war spokesman and Khomeini's personal representative on the Supreme Council, and was re-elected *Majlis* Speaker for the ninth successive year on June 7. Ayatollah Montazeri had unsuccessfully argued that he should relinquish this post so as to concentrate on co-ordinating the war effort. Rafsanjani's new appointment gave him the authority he needed to push through one of the regime's most controversial foreign policy decisions—the end of the war with Iraq.

Rafsanjani's hold on the military was strengthened by the dissolution of the Revolutionary Guards Ministry in July. Sections of the Guards were angry at public statements implicitly blaming them for military defeats. The former Minister, Moshen Rafiqdost, who had been implicated in alleged corrupt dealings in military equipment, was appointed as Rafsanjani's adviser in November.

Moussavi offered to resign in September, fearing that increasing political opposition might prevent him from continuing with his socialist-style economic policies and that the *Majlis* might reject some of his nominations for ministerial office. His offer was rejected by President Khamenei, while in a rare public rebuke, Ayatollah Khomeini told him that this was "no time for bickering and resigning". In practice, some of Moussavi's strongest supporters, including the Interior Minister, Hojatolislam Ali Akbar Mohtashemi, were accepted by the *Majlis* by only a narrow margin, while others favouring a more "open-door" economic and foreign policy, such as the Foreign Minister, Dr Ali Akbar Vellayati, secured their places by a comfortable margin.

In the wake of the war, Iran's economy was facing numerous difficulties. Damage to refineries combined with the sluggish state of the world oil market kept revenues depressed, while trade suffered as a result of the relatively weak US dollar (Iran's exports being largely denominated in dollars, its imports in other currencies). The country suffered from a foreign exchange shortage, and from growing unemployment (estimated as at least 20 per cent) and underemployment. Continuing rural migration to the cities adversely affected agricultural production; until recently self-sufficient in food, Iran was now importing US$2,000 million worth per year.

It emerged during late 1988 that Ahmad Khomeini, the Ayatollah's son, was becoming more influential, controlling all access to his father and supervising the Beit e-Imam, the Ayatollah's private office. Politically, Ahmad Khomeini appeared to be broadly aligned with Rafsanjani. Meanwhile, Ayatollah Montazeri appeared increasingly isolated, criticizing both Moussavi's economic policies and also the continuing abuse of human rights, against a background of reports of stepped-up executions of political prisoners and arrests of opponents of the prevailing government line. In an open letter to Moussavi, Ayatollah Montazeri claimed that "all the present shortcomings, discrimination, social injustice, low earnings of the deprived sectors of society and soaring prices are the natural consequences of the policies of your government . . . You cannot any longer use the excuse of war for the long queues for basic foodstuffs and ration coupons. It is time people were treated with respect". While thereby aligning himself broadly with Rafsanjani on the economic front, Montazeri's outspoken criticisms of human rights violations alienated him from most of the leadership's key figures. "We are not going to solve anything by torturing, imprisoning or executing our opponents", he wrote. "It is clear that these repressive policies have distanced people from the authorities . . . and resulted in our political isolation among the international community. Islam is based on principles of forgiveness and compassion, but we have yet to learn this from the Prophet's noble legacy".

By the end of November, over 30 clergy who supported Montazeri were reported to have been executed (although such reports were difficult to confirm), while others had been arrested, and Montazeri himself was said to have been effectively barred from the state-controlled media.

THE WAR WITH IRAQ

ORIGINS OF THE DISPUTE

Mounting tension between Iraq and Iran exploded into war in September 1980, when Iraqi forces overran large tracts of south-western Iran. The origins of the war lay in a long-standing dispute over the Shatt al-Arab ("Arab river") waterway, which runs into the Persian (Arabian) Gulf between the two countries and is formed by the confluence of the Tigris and Euphrates rivers. The area is of major economic importance to both countries, particularly since the development of their respective oil industries. Iran's major oil refinery was built at Abadan, while Iraq's main oil terminal was at Fao, with its principal port at Basra. From the north, the land border reaches the waterway some 60 miles from the coast, about 10 miles north of Khorramshahr.

The boundary between Persia (Iran) and the Turkish Ottoman Empire (which then controlled the area presently occupied by the state of Iraq) was originally delimited by the Treaty of Zuhab in 1639. Over the next 200 years, the precise border along the Shatt al-Arab area remained very vague, however, depending largely on the prevailing loyalty of the fiercely independent tribal rulers of the region. The exact border in this area was first defined in 1847 by a four-party boundary commission, comprising representatives of Russia and Britain (who both exercised considerable influence in the region at this time) in addition to Iran and Turkey. Under the Treaty of Ezerum, Iran was awarded the eastern bank of the river, including the towns of Mohammerah (now Khorramshahr) and Abadan, while Turkey retained sovereignty over the waterway itself. These provisions were never fully implemented, however, although by the end of the century the local inhabitants had reached an informal agreement by which the boundary was regarded as running down the middle of the river, with both sides controlling navigation.

In the early twentieth century, sovereignty over the Shatt al-Arab became an important issue for Iran with the growth of the port of Mohammerah and the discovery of oil in the area. Iran was particularly concerned at the fact that ships trading with Mohammerah and the new oil terminal at Abadan had to anchor in Turkish waters and pay Turkish import duties. This problem persisted after Iraq had become a British mandate following the defeat of the Ottoman Empire in the First World War. The British authorities set up a Basra port authority to supervise navigation and maintain essential services, paid for by levies on commercial shipping. Iran maintained that, in common with most riverine boundaries, the border should follow the "Thalweg principle" (whereby frontiers are defined as following the median line of the deepest channel). A compromise agreement reached in 1914 applied this principle to the river in the vicinity of Mohammerah; this was extended to Abadan in a treaty concluded in 1937, which also stipulated that ships using all other parts of the river should fly the Iraqi flag. Some provision was made for Iran to receive a share of the revenues raised from the river.

Iranian discontent with this arrangement surfaced again in the mid-1960s, when the Shah reiterated earlier claims that, while ships using Iranian ports contributed the bulk of revenues from the waterway, Iraq was neither using these funds to benefit the river's facilities nor allocating a share to Iran. In April 1969, Iran repudiated the 1937 treaty, and announced that its vessels would neither pay Iraqi tolls nor fly the Iraqi flag in the waterway. Iraq responded by declaring that the river was Iraqi territory and threatening action against any Iranian vessel contravening the terms of the treaty. Although it refrained from confrontation on the waterway, Iraq's relations with Iran steadily deteriorated. There was a series of border incidents in the early seventies as Iran supported Kurdish rebels fighting for autonomy in Iraq and occupied three disputed islands (Abu Musa, Greater and Little Tumb) in the Strait of Hormuz, leading Iraq to sever diplomatic relations in 1973. However, thanks to intervention by the UN Security Council and mediation by several other oil-exporting countries, the two sides signed a new treaty in June 1975 under which the river border would be drawn according to the Thalweg principle. Other outstanding border uncertainties were also cleared up by the treaty, which also provided for the establishment of border security arrangements to prevent the infiltration of undesirable elements from either direction.

ESCALATION OF TENSION AFTER IRANIAN REVOLUTION —OUTBREAK OF WAR

In the wake of the Iranian revolution, tension between the two countries escalated sharply. Iraq feared the influence of Iranian Shia fundamentalism on its own Shia populace, while Iran resented Iraqi support for the Arab minority of Khuzistan. In October 1979, Iraq issued a three-point declaration demanding the abrogation of the 1975 treaty and the restoration to Iraq of its former rights, the evacuation by Iran of the three islands in the Hormuz Strait and the granting of autonomy to Iran's Baluchi, Kurdish and Arab minorities. Iran rejected these demands as unwarranted interference in its internal affairs. Henceforth, relations deteriorated sharply. The two sides embarked on a propaganda war, each calling for the overthrow of the other's government and castigating each other as puppets of imperialism. After several minor clashes, heavy cross-border fighting erupted in July 1980 as Iraq seized portions of territory which it claimed had been illegally "usurped" by Iran in contravention of the 1975 treaty.

On Sept.17, 1980, President Saddam Hussein unilaterally abrogated the 1975 agreement and claimed that Iraq's sovereignty over the Shatt al-Arab had been restored. Four days later, Iraq launched a large-scale offensive which rapidly gained control of part of the province of Khuzistan, capturing Khorramshahr and encircling Abadan. Iraq also made gains further north. Oil installations in both countries suffered serious damage and ships in the Shatt al-Arab were blocked by the ferocity of the fighting. On Sept.24, Iraq demanded that, in return for a ceasefire, Iran should recognize Iraq's sovereignty over the Shatt al-Arab and the border area and return to Arab ownership the three islands in the Strait of Hormuz. Iran rejected these conditions. As fighting persisted, various Iraqi officials made other demands, including the claim that Iraq had a "historic" and "nationalist" right to the province of Khuzistan (referred to as "Arabistan" by Iraq). In the face of Iranian rejection of these damands, Iraq threatened to occupy more territory and forge closer ties with other minority groups.

Early mediation efforts by the UN, Islamic Conference and Non-Aligned Movement failed in the face of Iraqi insistence on Iranian territorial concessions and Iran's refusal to depart from the terms of the 1975 accord. The war continued sporadically through 1981, with the military position changing little from that reached in the early stages of the fighting, although Iran did succeed in lifting the siege of Abadan in September. The situation changed dramatically in March 1982, however, when Iran launched an aggressive counter-attack, driving the Iraqis back to the border and recapturing Khorramshahr. On this basis, the Iranian government proposed terms for a settlement which included payment of war reparations by Iraq and the removal of the Saddam Hussein government from power.

With Iraq now on the defensive, there was considerable speculation over the ensuing five years, fuelled by official Iranian statements, that Iran would launch a "final offensive" to end the war. No successful operation on such a scale emerged, however, as Iraq continued to benefit from diplomatic and financial support from many Arab states, and from increasingly sophisticated weapons supplies from the Soviet Union, France and other sources. Although there was no active intervention by other Arab armies, both Jordanian and Sudanese "volunteers" joined the Iraqi forces in limited numbers. For its part, Iran enjoyed some diplomatic support from Libya, Syria and several radical third-world governments, but was restricted to international and clandestine markets for its arms supplies. As Iran pressed home its advantage, meanwhile, both the USA and the Soviet Union began to favour Iraq, fearing the destabilizing consequences of an outright victory by the Islamic revolution. This stance was echoed by most Western states, many of whom, however, attempted to maintain cordial relations with both sides. In practice, this meant that they were effectively supplying both sides simultaneously with the means to prolong the bloodshed.

The vast majority of Arab states expressed varying degrees of support for Iraq. The Fez summit of Arab heads of state in 1982 praised what it termed Iraq's "withdrawal" from Iranian territory, and warned that "any aggression against an Arab country" would be considered as "aggression against all Arab countries". The Syrian government supported the resolution, thereby ending its open support for Iran.

Iran launched the first in a series of major offensives, code-named *Al Fajr* ("Dawn") in February 1983, in an effort to cut the Baghdad-Basra highway. The "human waves" of lightly-armed Iranian soldiers were beaten back by Iraqi forces using armour and air-strikes. While the Iranians suffered heavy casualties, the smaller Iraqi losses proved less sustainable, due to Iraq's inferiority in manpower. Iranian leaders continued to reject international appeals for a ceasefire, insisting on the overthrow of Saddam Hussein as the minimum condition for peace. Iranian forces made further gains in late 1983 in the mountainous border regions of north-eastern Iran, thereby cutting communications between Iraqi units and Iranian Kurdish fighters who had been assisting them as part of their own long-running guerrilla war against the Tehran government. At the end of 1983, Iran captured several key islands in the oil fields of the Majnoon marshes, just inside Iraq on the southern front.

At about this time, evidence began to emerge that Iraq was using chemical weapons, mostly forms of mustard gas akin to that used in Europe in the First World War. Examination of wounded Iranian soldiers confirmed the fact that such weapons were being deployed, and Iraq's use of them was specifically condemned in a UN Security Council resolution in March 1986.

In an effort to persuade Iran to agree to a ceasefire, the Iraqi Air Force flew repeated missions against Iranian oil installations, notably the Kharg island terminal, from mid-1983 onwards. The loan of French Super-Etendard aircraft equipped with Exocet anti-ship missiles enabled Iraq to strike at tankers travelling to and from Iranian oil terminals. In response, Iran threatened to "close the Gulf" to all shipping at the Strait of Hormuz, which in turn drew a warning from the US administration that it would ensure that the Gulf remained open. To this end, a US naval task force was stationed in the Straits area, part of a general build up of Western and Soviet-bloc navies in the region. From May 1984, Iran began retaliating by attacking tankers trading with Iraq's Gulf Arab allies, notably Saudi Arabia and Kuwait. This drew a condemnation from the UN Security Council, which demanded respect for the principle of freedom of navigation. Air attacks on industrial and civilian targets were also a regular feature of the war, continuing despite international appeals for a moratorium. They were suspended in June 1984 as a result of an initiative by Sr Pérez de Cuellar, the UN Secretary-General. Six months later, however, Iraq resumed the air raids, provoking retaliatory Iranian strikes. Iraq's air superiority enabled it to carry out raids deep into Iran, while the relative weakness of the Iranian Air Force forced it to rely on missile attacks.

In an attempt to achieve a decisive breakthrough against Iraq, the Iranians launched a major offensive in the central sector in March 1985, but their forces were repulsed with heavy casualties. Much of Iraq's defensive strategy in the region relied on the flooding of marshlands to impede the progress of Iranian infantry. The apparent failure of the "human wave" tactics fuelled increasing differences within the Iranian political and military leadership over both the wisdom of attempting such costly operations and also the viability of any planned "final offensive". Some officials started to speak of the overriding strategy as being that of a "defensive *jihad*". In November, Iran's Foreign Minister Ali Akbar Vellayati held talks on possible peaceful solutions to the conflict with King Fahd of Saudi Arabia (one of Iraq's closest allies). As international mediation efforts continued, the UN Security Council passed a resolution in February 1986 which "deplored the initial acts which gave rise to the conflict". Although this did not mention Iraq by name, it was seen as going some way towards Iran's demand that the Iraqi regime should be condemned and "punished" as the aggressor.

In the sea war, both sides escalated strikes on oil tankers and merchant shipping, with over 130 tankers being attacked in 1985–86. In September 1985 Iran began to stop and search vessels suspected of supplying military equipment to Iraq, among them US and Soviet craft. French, British and US ships responded by stepping up patrols in the southern Gulf. Iraq's attacks on oil installations became increasingly effective during 1986–87 as pilots adopted low-level bombing tactics. By the end of 1986, Western experts were estimating that Iran's refined oil exports had been cut by half.

Iranian ground forces scored a significant victory early in 1986 when a sophisticated commando operation overwhelmed Iraqi defences at the deserted port of Fao. A year later, the Iranians captured several islands in the Shatt al-Arab during an offensive aimed at capturing Basra. For a time it looked as though the city might fall, but the attack was halted after Iranian leaders declared that its purpose was to "destroy the Iraqi war machine" rather than make territorial gains. An element of Iran's success in the operation was attributed to the recent arrival of US weapons and spare parts, delivered as part of the secret "arms-for-hostages" arrangement, details of which emerged during late 1986. In particular, the availability of modern anti-tank missiles was thought to have hampered counter-attacks by Iraqi armoured units. Iranian forces also scored limited successes in the central and northern sector, while Iraq responded by stepping up the air raids in the "war of the cities", although both sides agreed to a further moratorium in February 1987.

In a further effort to satisfy Iranian diplomatic demands, Pérez de Cuellar, in January 1987, proposed the creation of an international panel to determine war guilt. The Iranian government failed to respond, and launched further land attacks in April.

Attempting to gain some protection from Iranian attacks on its vessels, Kuwait, in April 1987, chartered three Soviet-registered tankers, which would automatically become entitled to Soviet naval protection. The move did not prevent the ships coming under attack, however. In a more serious incident, over 37 US crewmen on board the USS *Stark*, on patrol near the entrance to the Gulf, were killed on May 17 when the ship was struck by two Exocet missiles fired by an Iraqi aircraft. Although Iraq later apologized for its "mistake", the action was widely seen as a ploy to draw the USA deeper into the conflict. If this was the case, it was successful. US naval presence in the Gulf was increased, and fleets of Kuwaiti tankers were re-registered under the US flag. Iran at this time resorted to laying mines in the Gulf shipping lanes, causing damage to several tankers, and stepped up machine-gun and rocket attacks on vessels trading with Iraq and Arab Gulf states. This in turn led to a number of Western European nations sending minesweepers and naval escort vessels to help protect their shipping. During September, Iran fired several Chinese-supplied Silkworm missiles at Kuwaiti oil installations, apparently as a warning to Kuwait to stop supporting Iraq. Other attacks followed in early 1988.

Tension rose in September when US helicopters attacked an Iranian landing craft which had been laying mines north of Bahrain. In October, US helicopters sank three Iranian patrol craft while destroyers shelled oil platforms which were believed to be used as bases by revolutionary guards for attacks on shipping. The USA carried out further attacks on Iranian vessels and oil platforms in April 1988, after a US frigate had been damaged by a mine believed to have been laid by Iranian units. In what appeared to be a genuine mistake, the cruiser USS *Vincennes* shot down an Iranian civil airliner over the Gulf on a flight to Dubai on July 3, 1988, with the loss of 290 lives.

RENEWED IRAQI VICTORIES—IRANIAN ACCEPTANCE OF CEASEFIRE

After a period of intensive diplomatic contact, the UN Security Council on July 20, 1987, unanimously adopted Resolution 598, which called for a ceasefire, withdrawal to internationally-recognized borders, exchange of prisoners and commencement of peace negotiations. As a sop to Iran's demands that Iraq should be blamed for the war, the resolution provided for "an impartial body", which would be "entrusted with the task of inquiring into responsibility for the conflict". It also contained implicit provision for an arms embargo "to ensure compliance with the resolution". The Iraqi government immediately accepted 598, on condition that Iran did likewise. For their part, Iranian leaders avoided outright rejection of it, but described it as "unjust", and continued to demand the overthrow of President Hussein.

The military advantage, however, was beginning to slip from Iran's grasp. A major planned offensive against Iraqi positions in front of Basra had to be called off in early 1988 when it became clear that Iran could not mobilize sufficient volunteers to mount the operation. Its forces did, however, make further gains in Iraqi Kurdistan during March, with the assistance of Kurdish rebels fighting the Baghdad regime. In response, however, Iraq used chemical weapons to bomb Kurdish towns and villages, killing over 5,000 people, mostly civilians.

By April 1988, Iran's armed forces were suffering from a severe shortage of arms and ammunition, as international pressure, notably from the USA and the Soviet Union, restricted the availability of suitable supplies on the private market. In particular, Iranian armoured units were crippled by a shortage of spare parts and ammunition, and there was also a lack of artillery shells and ammunition for recoilless rifles, the infantry's principal weapon against Iraqi armour. In the first of a series of major victories which culminated in Iran's agreeing to a ceasefire, Iraqi troops on April 18 re-captured Fao, which had fallen to the Iranians two years previously. They moved on to recover ground around Shalamcheh in May, captured during an Iranian assault in January 1987. In both cases, the Iranian positions were only lightly defended by youthful or middle-aged "basiji" volunteers. An Iranian counter-offensive failed to press home initial gains. Iraqi armoured units succeeded in driving out-gunned Iranian forces from the southern Iraqi marshlands in June, and there were also significant Iraqi victories in Kurdistan. Several Iranian border towns in the southern and central sectors were also briefly occupied by Iraqi troops.

Iraqi attacks were accompanied by thrusts across the central front by the *Mujaheddin's* "National Liberation Army" (NLA), which, with Iraqi logistical support, advanced 100 km into Iran in the direction of Kermanshah in July, before withdrawing in the face of Iranian counter-attacks. The NLA had hoped to be welcomed by the populace as liberators, but their harsh treatment of local officials in towns they captured alienated potential support. Large numbers of NLA fighters were reportedly killed after being trapped by Iranian forces.

As the Iranian military response to the renewed Iraqi offensives wavered, internal opposition to the war within Iran increased, with a number of leading clerics pleading with Ayatollah Khomeini "to end the conflict with honour". Although both President Khamenei and Khomeini himself rejected peace talks, the appointment of Rafsanjani as Commander-in-Chief in June heightened the chances of Iran accepting a peaceful settlement. Announcing the formation of a "unified military command", to be composed of representatives of the government, army and revolutionary guards, on July 2, Rafsanjani declared his willingness to pursue a "non-military option" as a means of ending the war. On July 18, a statement issued in the name of the "General Command HQ", announced that Iran accepted Resolution 598 "in the interests of security and on the basis of justice". The statement complained bitterly of widespread foreign support for Iraq, claiming that "an international conspiracy of arrogance and reaction" had sustained the Iraqi war effort "with a flood of military, financial and political-propaganda assistance".

Iran's acceptance of the ceasefire led to a swift end to the fighting, with most clashes being over within a week, and a slow start to peace negotiations, with precious little tangible progress being made over the ensuing six months. The Iranian decision had apparently been taken on

July 16 at a meeting of the regime's leading officials, including Rafsanjani, President Khamenei, and members of the Assembly of Experts, Council of Guardians and Supreme Judicial Council. Acceptance of the ceasefire had reportedly been strongly advocated by Rafsanjani and the Foreign Minister, Dr Vellayati, and opposed in particular by Ayatollah Montazeri. Ayatollah Khomeini himself did not take part in the meeting, and was informed of the decision after it had been taken, apparently confirming the impression that he no longer played a key role in Iranian decision-making. In his first statement on the ceasefire, made on July 20, Khomeini told the Iranian public that "taking this decision was more deadly for me than taking poison".

FOREIGN AFFAIRS

INITIAL IMPACT OF THE REVOLUTION

The revolutionary regime established on Feb.11, 1979, was formally recognized within days by many of Iran's neighbouring states, including Iraq and Saudi Arabia, as well as the Soviet Union, China, the United Kingdom and most third-world nations. Egypt and the United States, which had been among the Shah's strongest supporters, both offered de facto recognition. The regime's first Foreign Minister, Dr Sanjabi, promised that Iran's foreign policy would in future be based on independence and non-alignment, and that it was ready to have friendly relations with Western and Soviet-bloc countries.

One exception was Israel. A week after the revolution, Tehran severed relations with Israel, and paid host to a visit by the PLO leader Yasser Arafat. A PLO spokesman subsequently stated that the new regime had made "the liberation of Jerusalem from Israeli occupation one of its foremost religious and moral commitments". Relations with Egypt were severed in April, as a mark of protest against the Camp David peace treaty with Israel. In early March, the Chief of Staff announced that the Iranian contingent of the United Nations Interim force in Lebanon (UNIFIL) would be withdrawn because Iran was "now one of the confrontation states against Israel". The 5,000-strong Iranian expeditionary corps in Oman, which had helped guard against the infiltration of left-wing guerrillas from South Yemen, was withdrawn, and the government announced that Iran would no longer be playing the role of "policeman of the Persian Gulf".

In a foretaste of its commitment to export its revolution, Dr Ibrhaim Yazdi, Deputy Prime Minister in charge of Revolutionary Affairs, declared on Feb.25 that "the success of the Islamic revolution in Iran has shown our Arab neighbours that Islam provides the ideological basis for change within

Moslem countries and that it can also replace Arab nationalism as a rallying point for the Arab people. . . . From now on, all Islamic movements which were dormant or apologetic in their approach to change or action will come out in the open".

The other early diplomatic casualty of the revolution was South Africa, which had imported 90 per cent of its oil requirements from the Shah's sanction-busting regime. The Iranians severed relations on March 4, and confirmed that in future no oil would be exported to South Africa.

THE UNITED STATES

Faced with the downfall of one of its greatest regional allies, the US Administration announced on Feb.9, 1979, that it would "attempt to work closely with the new regime". Such hopes were to prove fruitless, however. In the months following the revolution, the Iranians took steps to end all military co-operation, including closing down the US surveillance posts on the Soviet border and rescinding all arms-purchasing contracts, with the exception of spare parts. Increasingly hostile coverage in the American media, notably over reports of human rights violations, was matched by growing anti-US propaganda from the Iranian leadership. On May 17, the US Senate unanimously adopted a resolution expressing indignation at the summary executions taking place in Iran. Two weeks later, the Iranian government rejected the US administration's nomination for its new ambassador to Tehran, and the post was left unfilled. To some extent, the new regime was divided over its attitude to the USA, with Dr Bazargan's government attempting, largely unsuccessfully, to maintain workable relations, while the radical-dominated Revolutionary Council was against any compromise with the "Great Satan".

Relations worsened dramatically in October when, contrary to earlier US assurances, the former Shah was allowed into the USA for cancer treatment. The move came despite warnings from both the Central Intelligence Agency and embassy staff in Tehran that the Shah's presence in the USA could trigger violent anti-Americanism in Iran and provoke an attack on the embassy, which had already been occupied briefly by *Fedayeen-e Khalq* members just after the revolution on Feb.14. These worst fears were realized on Nov.4, when a group of armed militants, describing themselves as "students", seized control of the embassy and took the staff hostage, offering to release them only on condition that the US government extradited the Shah to face trial in Iran. Five women and 13 black men were released on the orders of Ayatollah Khomeini on Nov.17; the remaining 52 were kept in spartan conditions and repeatedly threatened with being put on trial as spies. Separate efforts to secure their release by US and PLO emissaries came to nothing, although it emerged increasingly that sections of the government (as opposed to revolutionary) leadership were in favour of an early release in return for limited concessions from the USA.

The UN Security Council unanimously called on Iran to release the hostages on Nov.9. A similar resolution was approved by consensus in the UN's General Assembly in early December. The initial US response to the hostage seizure included a halt to the shipment of US$300 million worth of military spare parts already paid for by Tehran and a ban on US oil imports from Iran. On Nov.14, President Carter issued an executive order freezing all Iranian government assets in the USA, which were believed to total some US$6,000 million. While rejecting calls for military action against Iran by right-wing politicians, the US administration also took steps to reinforce its naval presence off the Iranian coast. The freeze on assets was welcomed by President Bani-Sadr as "an unexpected gift" which would "free Iran from the economic, cultural and psychological grip of the USA". Bani-Sadr later said that Iran would refuse to pay its foreign debts (estimated at US$15,000 million) as they had been incurred as a result of the activities of "looters and foreign collaborators".

While America's Western allies strongly supported its stance over the crisis, the Soviet Union and some third-world states drew a distinction between the hostage-taking, which they denounced as violating international law, and the increasingly bellicose US response, which they saw as provocative and threatening.

After an unsuccessful visit to Tehran by the UN Secretary-General, Dr Kurt Waldheim, the USA submitted a resolution to the UN Security Council in January 1980 envisaging drastic sanctions against Iran. This was vetoed by the Soviet Union. In an effort to resolve the crisis, a UN team commission of inquiry travelled to Iran in February to hear the grievances of the Iranian people against the former Shah, who had by now left the United States for a temporary refuge in Panama, from where he travelled to Egypt in March to take up President Sadat's long-standing offer of a permanent home. This effectively ended the efforts of moderate Iranian leaders to initiate extradition proceedings in Panama, which could be portrayed as sufficient reason to release the US hostages. The UN commission made little progress, however, in the light of widely differing interpretations being placed on its work by Iran and the USA, and at the end of February, Ayatollah Khomeini ruled that the fate of the hostages would be determined by the next session of the *Majlis*.

Intense diplomatic activity continued during March, as the USA in particular sought to exploit the differences between the radicals on the revolutionary council and President Bani-Sadr's relatively moderate approach. When these came to nothing, however, the USA severed diplomatic relations and imposed tougher economic sanctions. Under considerable US pressure, the European Community's Council of Ministers approved a package of limited diplomatic and economic sanctions on April 22, with stronger measures to follow if the hostages were not released. Other countries, including Canada, Australia and Japan, followed suit. Before the sanctions had time to take effect, however, the USA mounted a complex rescue mission which ended in disaster.

The plan provided for 90 US commandos to be flown in Hercules C-130 transport aircraft to a disused airstrip near Tabas, 380 miles south of Tehran, from where they would fly by eight helicopters to a second hideout at Damavand, 30 miles east of the capital. Here they would meet up with Iranian agents and travel to Tehran in trucks, securing the embassy compound, which would already have been infiltrated by other agents, by using nerve gas to incapacitate the guards. The helicopters from Damavand would then arrive to evacuate the hostages and commandos. However, two of the helicopters, including one carrying vital hydraulic repair equipment, broke down before reaching Tabas. Once at the airstrip, a third helicopter was discovered to have suffered hydraulic failure. Since six was the minimum number deemed sufficient for the mission, the rescue plan was then abandoned. While attempting to refuel prior to evacuating, a fourth helicopter crashed into a transport aircraft. Both aircraft burst into flames, killing eight commandos. The remaining helicopters were abandoned for fear of shrapnel damage from the explosion, and the remaining commandos were evacuated by the Hercules. Addressing jubilant crowds celebrating the news of the rescue mission's failure, Iranian leaders claimed that God had been on their side in inflicting a defeat on the "Great Satan".

In the wake of the failed mission, diplomatic negotiations continued, with progress being aided by the death of the Shah on July 27. The deadlock was eventually broken as a result of intensive mediation by the Algerian government. The hostages were transferred by the students to government control on Nov.3 after a special *Majlis* commission had announced conditions for their release. The Iranian willingness to reach an agreement was seen in part as a reaction to the outbreak of the Gulf War. The hostages were finally released on Jan.20, 1981, after the signature of an accord in which the USA undertook not to interfere in Iran's internal affairs, to freeze the assets of the Shah's family in the USA (pending resolution of the Iranian government's lawsuit to recover the wealth), while releasing Iranian assets frozen at the start of the crisis, to end all trade sanctions against Iran and agree to the setting up of an international tribunal to decide all claims of US citizens against Iran and vice-versa. The incoming Reagan administration duly lifted sanctions, along with other US allies. It was widely agreed that the sanctions had had little practical effect,with Iran's needs being imported through "neutral" countries. The international tribunal handed down a ruling in July 1986 requiring the USA to pay Iran US$500 million as compensation for Iranian interest payments on syndicated bank loans.

In the years following the hostage seizure, the USA increasingly favoured Iraq in the Gulf War, particularly after Iran gained the initiative in 1982. The CIA stepped up clandestine support to the exiled Iranian opposition after the October 1983 bombing of the US peacekeeping force's HQ in Beirut, in the belief that the Iranian government was partly behind the action. Iran was placed on the State Department's list of "terrorist nations" in January 1984, shortly after Iraq had been removed from it. US spokesmen assured Gulf Arab states of its support for Iraq as "the first line of defence against Iranian expansionism", and reliable reports indicated that Iraq's repulsion of repeated Iranian offensives was assisted by US satellite intelligence information. Iranian threats to close the Straits of Hormuz were met with repeated US warnings that it would take all necessary steps to keep the Gulf open.

A dramatic turn in Iranian-US relations was revealed in late 1986, when it emerged that, in an effort to win the confidence of certain supposedly sympathetic Iranian leaders, and thereby secure the release of kidnap victims held by pro-Iranian groups in Lebanon, members of the President's National Security Council (NSC) had embarked in 1985 on a secret policy of selling arms to Iran. Revenue from the arms sales was subsequently diverted to the Nicaraguan "contra" guerrillas at a time when such assistance was banned by US law. The revelations caused a major political storm in the USA, focusing on the fact that NSC officials, notably Lt.-Col. Oliver North, together with Adml. John Poindexter, the President's National Security Adviser, and his predecessor, Mr Robert McFarlane, had effectively attempted to conduct a separate foreign policy beyond the scrutiny of Congress and largely without the knowledge of the State and Defense Departments. The operation was believed to have been actively encouraged by the CIA director, William Casey, who died in May 1987 without having given evidence to either the Tower commission of inquiry appointed by the President, or the subsequent congressional hearings, at which most of the US protagonists gave evidence. The extent of involvement of President Reagan and Vice-President George Bush was uncertain, although it was generally accepted that they had not been aware of all aspects of the operation.

US involvement in the transfer of arms to Iran had begun in the summer of 1985 with the delivery of two consignments of anti-tank missiles from stocks held by Israel. A significant role in initiating and financing the sales was played by a number of semi-independent international arms dealers, including Adnan Khashoggi, a Saudi Arabian (acting, on some accounts, with tacit backing from the Saudi leadership, which reportedly had reservations about its previous unambiguous support for Iraq), Manucher Ghorbanifar, an Iranian, and Al Schwimmer, an Israeli arms manufacturer and informal adviser to Israel's Prime Minister, Shimon Peres. Also involved was Michael Ledeen, an NSC consultant on Iran who had political connections in Israel. Detailed operational control was in the hands of Col. North, who recruited Maj.-Gen. Richard Secord, a retired US Air Force officer with extensive knowledge of Iran, and his Iranian-born business partner, Albert Hakim. These three, together with Adml. Poindexter, were indicted on charges of conspiracy, fraud, obstruction and embezzlement in March 1988, although the most serious charges against North were subsequently dropped due to the Reagan administration's refusal to release classified documents required by the prosecution. The identity of contacts on the Iranian side was somewhat obscure, but they were known to include Hojatolislam Rafsanjani, Hossein Moussavi and Ahmed Khomeini.

The first consignments reportedly helped secure the release of one of the Beirut captives, Rev. Benjamin Weir. Further shipments followed a trip to Tehran in May 1986 by McFarlane and North, accompanied by Amiram Nir, Peres's adviser on terrorism. During their stay, revolutionary guards repelled an attack on their hotel by a dissident faction loyal to Ayatollah Montazeri. McFarlane made a further visit in September. Two other Beirut hostages, Lawrence Jenco and David Jacobsen, were released in July and November 1986. The deliveries were halted after the story broke.

Although radical anti-American factions in Iran sought to use the incident to damage the standing of Rafsanjani and other "pragmatists", these justified the deals as a means of acquiring weapons badly needed for the war front, while stressing the political discomfiture which the revelation of the operation had caused in the USA. Renewed tension resulted from the US build-up in the Gulf during 1987–88 and the shooting down of the Iranian airliner (see p. 49), and there were allegations that radical elements opposed to Rafsanjani were responsible for the bombing of the US airliner which crashed over Scotland in December 1988.

Canada's relations with Iran, which were severed in 1980 after Canadian diplomats helped six US embassy staff to flee the country, were eventually renewed in July 1988.

WESTERN EUROPE AND JAPAN

Iran's relations with Western Europe (covered in detail in Sir Anthony Parsons' briefing, below) also suffered as a result of the revolution, but less dramatically so than those with the USA. **France's** relations with the new regime initially looked promising, in the light of Khomeini's short period of exile in Paris immediately before his return to Tehran. However, French tolerance of opposition exile activity, notably by Massoud Rajavi's *Mujaheddin* and ex-President Bani-Sadr, severely strained relations in the early 1980s, and this was compounded by open French support for Iraq, backed up by arms supplies. French banks in Iran lost their special status, French products were boycotted and the size of the embassy reduced. Diplomatic relations were severed in July 1987, after allegations that Iran had been behind bomb attacks in Paris, but were renewed the following year amid reports that France had agreed to scale down military support for Iraq and make a series of payments in return for the release of two French hostages held by a pro-Iranian group in Beirut.

The **United Kingdom's** support for the US administration put relations with Iran under strain, although the storming of the London embassy in May 1980 by SAS commandos freeing staff taken hostage was appreciated in Iran. Relations worsened in 1985–87 over the detention of a British businessman in Tehran on spying charges, the arrest for shoplifting of an Iranian diplomat in Manchester, and the apparent retaliatory beating up of a British diplomat. In common with other Western countries, the end of the Gulf War, and consequent opportunities for European companies to participate in reconstruction work, led to a gradual improvement in relations between Iran and the UK. An agreement on compensation payments for damage to diplomatic property was reached in July 1988, to be followed by an undertaking to restore full diplomatic relations, although the British made clear that this would be hampered by Iran's failure to secure the release of British hostages in Beirut.

West Germany kept up good commercial relations with the new regime. The Foreign Minister, Herr Hans-Dietrich Genscher, made an official visit to Iran in July 1984. Irritation at West Germany's tolerance of exiled opposition activity led to an attack on its Tehran embassy in October 1986, and two German diplomats were expelled in February 1987 as a protest against a satirical TV programme, described by Mr Moussavi as a "hostile action" which reflected "the racist and facist policies" of the West German government. Genscher paid a further visit to Tehran in November 1988, seeking to boost economic co-operation and also pressurize Iran to use its influence to free the Beirut hostages.

Iranian sensitivity over European satire also led to problems with the **Austrian** and **Italian** governments. Italian firms had secured a number of lucrative contracts in the early 1980s, notably in the oil industry, while Italy was the second biggest buyer of Iranian oil after Japan. Other European countries maintained good trading relations with Iran after the resolution of the US embassy hostage crisis, while keeping their distance politically and tending to favour Iraq in the Gulf War. During 1987, the UK, France, Italy, Belgium and the Netherlands all sent naval task forces, including minesweeping vessels, to the Gulf to help protect their shipping against Iranian attack.

The **Japanese** government enjoyed extensive commercial relations with Iran, which continued unabated after the revolution, although Japan did join the EC in imposing limited sanctions following the US hostage seizure. Some of the more lucrative Japanese contracts, notably the construction of a petrochemical plant at Bandar Khomeini, were suspended due to the Gulf War.

SOVIET UNION AND EASTERN EUROPE

The **Soviet Union** initially gave its broad approval to what it saw as an "anti-imperialist" revolution in Iran, particularly since the new regime had, the backing of the communist Tudeh Party. It went so far as to advise pro-Soviet Iranian leftists to support Khomeini's rule. Relations deteriorated sharply after the Soviet invasion of Afghanistan in December 1979, condemned as "a hostile measure against all the Moslems of the world", by Iranian leaders. By now, Khomeini himself was stressing that the Islamic revolution supported "neither East nor West . . . we are enemies of international communism". Iran joined the boycott of the 1980 Moscow Olympics. Despite these strains, trade between the two countries increased, with 15 per cent of Iran's imports being supplied by the Soviet Union in 1981 (in contrast to around five per cent under the Shah). At the outset of the Gulf War, the Soviet Union declared a position of neutrality, and stopped selling arms to Iraq. Moscow changed its stance after Iranian forces invaded Iraq in 1982, and resumed arms supplies, including ground-to-ground missiles which devastated Iranian towns from December 1982 onwards. Relations slumped still further after Iran banned the Tudeh Party in May 1983, expelled 18 Soviet diplomats and launched a campaign "on behalf of the oppressed Moslems of the Soviet Union". It also stepped up its support of the Afghan resistance.

Matters began to improve in 1984–85, with an exchange of official visits and an undertaking by Dr Vellayati "to increase and expand our relations". A visit by Georgy Kornienko, the highest-ranking Soviet official to visit the

Islamic Republic, in February 1986 culminated in an agreement to set up a joint commission on economic co-operation. In December of that year, the two sides signed a wide-ranging economic protocol providing for the return of Soviet technicians to work in Iran. By 1988, Iran was effectively playing a mediating role between the Soviet Union, currently withdráwing its troops from Afghanistan, and the divided Afghan resistance.

Other Eastern European states by and large followed the Soviet lead, and experienced some success in building up economic ties with the new regime. Iran and **Romania** signed a barter agreement providing for the sale of oil in exchange for foodstuffs totalling over US$1,000 million in October 1981. **East Germany's** trade with Iran increased four-fold after the revolution, while **Czechoslovakia** and **Hungary** secured contracts to develop Iran's power generation and agriculture respectively.

ARAB STATES AND THE THIRD WORLD

The **Arab Gulf states** viewed the Islamic revolution with suspicion, fearing with good reason that it would encourage their own disadvantaged Shia communities to take up revolutionary cudgels at home. In the wake of the seizure by militant Shia groups of the Grand Mosque in Mecca (Saudi Arabia) in November 1979, sympathetic demonstrators in other Saudi towns chanted slogans supporting Khomeini. Iranian spokesmen at various times denounced the Gulf's monarchs as un-Islamic, and called for their overthrow. The antagonism deepened after the outbreak of war, with the Gulf states giving moral and financial support to Iraq, and Iran issuing thinly-veiled threats to extend the war to their own soil (see p. 49). Iran gave support to the Organization of the Islamic Revolution in the Arab Peninsula (active in Saudi Arabia) and the Islamic League of Bahraini students. A coup plot foiled by the Bahraini security forces in January 1982 was blamed on Iran. A group of Iranian infiltrators was arrested on landing in Kuwait in October 1983; subsequent discoveries of anti-government plots in Kuwait and Bahrain led to further allegations of Iranian involvement, as did the series of bomb attacks in Kuwait City in December 1983.

One effect of the Islamic revolution was to draw the Gulf states closer together, and, as a group, closer to the USA. The formation in 1981 of the Gulf Co-operation Council (GCC—comprising Bahrain, Kuwait, Oman, Qatar, Saudi Arabia and the United Arab Emirates) arose out of the perceived need to stand together against the Iranian threat. After counter-attacking Iranian troops crossed into Iraq in 1982, Saudi Arabia warned of the possibility of "no holds barred" war with Iran, and in November a summit meeting of GCC heads of state declared that "Iran's trespassing over the Iraqi border endangers the safety of the Arab nation". The GCC states became increasingly embroiled in the Gulf War from May 1984 onwards, when Iran started to take revenge for Iraqi attacks on its tankers and oil terminals by targeting ships trading with Iraq's Gulf allies. In the only direct military confrontation, Saudi F-15 fighters intercepted and shot down at least one Iranian F-4 off the Saudi coast in June 1984.

Trade across the Gulf continued, however, despite the political tension. Dubai, one of the United Arab Emirates, in particular enjoyed strong commercial links with Iranian ports. From the mid-1980s onwards, both sides attempted to put relations on a more even keel. Partly thanks to mediation by Syria, which enjoyed good relations with both countries, Saudi Arabia and Iran effected a degree of rapprochement in May 1985 with a visit to Tehran by Prince Saud al Faisal, the Saudi Foreign Minister. During a return visit by Dr Vellayati in December, King Fahd spoke of the Saudi government's respect for Iran and its leaders, and declared his belief that the Shah's regime had neglected Islam. For his part, Vellayati said that Iran favoured "peaceful coexistence" with its Gulf neighbours. Similar sentiments had been expressed during a tour of Bahrain, Qatar and the UAE in October by an Iranian Deputy Foreign Minister, after which the Crown Prince of Qatar, Shaikh Hamad al Thani, had stated that "we admire Iran as a country in the forefront of struggle with Israel". The following year, the UAE's volume of trade with Iran reached a record US$1,000 million.

Relations took a turn for the worse in August 1987, however, with the deaths of several hundred Iranians during clashes with Saudi security forces in Mecca. Iranians participating in the annual pilgrimage (*haj*) to Mecca had regularly staged political demonstrations, shouting slogans denouncing Israel, the USA and Soviet Union, and, by implication, the pro-Western leaders of the Gulf kingdoms. On this occasion, however, the demonstration got out of hand, and in the ensuing fighting and stampedes, around 300 Iranians and a number of Saudis and pilgrims of other nationalities were killed. In retaliation, mobs attacked the Saudi and Kuwaiti embassies in Tehran. Iranian leaders again called for the overthrow of the Saudi regime and for the "freeing of the holy shrines [of Mecca and Medina] from the mischievous and wicked Wahabis" (the minority Moslem sect to which the Saudi royal family belonged). For the first time, a Saudi spokesman retaliated by calling for the overthrow of the Iranian regime. Diplomatic relations were eventually severed by Saudi Arabia in April 1988, after Iran had rejected demands to cut its number of pilgrims by two-thirds and refrain from any political demonstrations during the *haj*.

After the Gulf War ceasefire, Iran took steps to improve relations with the Arab Gulf states. Agreements to restore diplomatic relations were reached with Kuwait and Bahrain, and Iranian officials made numerous trips across the Gulf in an effort to forge closer ties and end the state of virtual cold war which had prevailed over most of the past decade.

Of the other Arab states, the Khomeini regime forged closest ties with the more radical "confrontational" states, notably **Libya**, with whom it restored diplomatic relations in November 1979, and **Syria**, which shared its antipathy towards Iraq, and also **South Yemen** and **Algeria**. Syrian aircraft provided cover for Iranian bombing raids on an Iraqi air base in April 1981. In March 1982, the two countries signed a 10-year trade agreement by which Syria would import Iranian oil in return for cash and bartered goods. Syria also allowed the passage of Iranian revolutionary guards into the Lebanese Bekaa Valley. For its part, Libya concluded a military co-operation agreement during a visit to Tripoli by Rafsanjani in June 1985, in which the two sides agreed to establish a (somewhat symbolic) "Army of Jerusalem to liberate Palestine".

By and large, however, Iran was isolated from the Arab world by its decision to pursue the Gulf War even after driving the Iraqis off its soil, and by its commitment to overthrow the Iraqi President. In addition, its relationship with Syria was strained over fighting in Lebanon between the Iranian-backed *Hezbollah* and the Syrian-supported Amal militias. Iran also maintained its position of unwavering hostility towards Egypt while the vast majority of Arab states were effecting a rapprochement with Cairo. Iran's isolation was brought home by the Arab League summit of November 1987. The final communique, endorsed unanimously, proclaimed the Arab world's solidarity with Iraq in the face of Iranian aggression, and blamed the Iranian pilgrims for the "bloody criminal acts" perpetrated during the *haj* in Mecca the previous August.

Despite enormous political differences, the Islamic Republic attempted to maintain working relations with its two other Islamic neighbours, Turkey and Pakistan. Trade with **Turkey** increased substantially in the early 1980s, partly at the expense of EC countries. Iran agreed to supply natural gas to Turkey in 1982, and by 1984, when the Prime Minister, Türgut Özal, visited Tehran, Turkey was Iran's third biggest trading partner after Japan and West Germany. Plans were laid for the construction of an oil pipeline from the Ahwaz oilfield to the Turkish port of Dörtyol. During 1987–88, however, there were several reported incidents of Iranian troops "accidentally" crossing into Turkey in the course of operations against Iraq and rebel Kurds, but these did no lasting harm to relations.

Gen. Zia's **Pakistan**, which was indebted to Iran to the tune of several thousand million US dollars, was at first denounced by radical elements as a lackey of the United States which had abandoned true Islam. Addressing a group of visiting Pakistani naval officers in November 1979, Khomeini called on them to instigate an Islamic revolution at home. The Soviet invasion of Afghanistan the following month, however, forged a strong bond of common interest between Pakistan and Iran, both of whom provided assistance and refuge to the Afghan guerrillas.

The Revolution's foreign policy (*Nick Danziger*)

A child of the Revolution (*Nick Danziger*)

PART II:

EXPERT BRIEFINGS
REPORTAGE
REFERENCE SECTION

1. IRAN AND ISLAM

Baqer Moin

The average Westerner's impression of Iran and Islam is based on sensational articles in the tabloid press and occasional TV news items which identify them with hostage taking, war and the abuse of human rights. Similarly, the average Iranian has a distorted view of the West. Britain and the United States are synonymous with imperialism, moral corruption, and exploitation of the Third World. Both of these views can be explained by Iran's past association with the West and the overwhelming Western influence in political and social affairs which has assailed the country since the mid-nineteenth century. In this respect at least, the resurgence of Islamic fundamentalism can be seen as a rejection of foreign domination.

The Iranian clergy have, over the years, felt threatened and betrayed, particularly as a result of three key developments in recent history: i) the outcome of the Constitutional Revolution of 1906–7, which sought to curb the monarch's absolute power. The clergy played a leading role in that movement, but were outmanoeuvred by secular forces, both of them losing out in the process; ii) the decline of the Ottoman Caliphate, and the placing of Iraq under British mandate, which in turn led to the emigration of some clergymen from Iraq and the expulsion or imprisonment of others; iii) The rise of Reza Shah and his anticlerical policies.

Having witnessed the destruction of Islamic institutions under Mostafa Kemal Ataturk's secular Turkish Republic, the Shia clergy did their best to prevent such an eventuality in Iran. When Reza Khan sought to replace the decaying Qajar dynasty with a republic, the clergy played a major role in maintaining the monarchical system and establishing the Pahlavi dynasty. After feeling betrayed by their secular allies following the Constitutional Revolution, the clergy were hoping that Reza Shah would keep his word "to uphold the precepts of holy religion". After making use of the clergy to consolidate his position, however, Reza Shah embarked on a similar plan to that of Ataturk, curtailing their power, depriving them of their social role and confining them to religious centres. The main body of the clergy in the theological centres went through a period of soul-searching quietism.

This was at a time when events were passing them by very fast. The modernization of the educational system, particularly the establishment of universities, meant that the clergy no longer had a monopoly over education. The secular right was given a relatively free reign to propagate nationalism, while the left, inspired and encouraged by the Soviet Union, was active in recruiting new members, who a decade later turned out to be the dominant force among the Iranian intellectuals. Had it not been for the over-ambitious policies of Reza Shah, who during the Second World War brought about the wrath of the Allies by his support for Nazi Germany, we might be writing about the clergy in Iran as a minor institution and not as a dominant political force.

When the Allies invaded Iran and toppled Reza Shah, religious and political freedom once again prevailed in Iran. But the main body of the clergy was more introverted, and out of touch with the ideological battles of the real world. The fall of Reza Shah brought about a period of political activity in the country with secular forces, both right and left, dominating the national political scene. It was against this background in 1944 that Ayatollah Khomeini—at the time a theological teacher in the holy city of Qom—first appeared on the scene, publishing a rebuff to an anti-clerical booklet. Driven by anger and frustration arising from the days of Reza Shah, Khomeini denounced the monarch and his policies, referring to him as "that illiterate soldier". Contrary to earlier generations of clergymen who were led to believe that democracy and constitutionalism in the Western sense was compatible with Islam, Khomeini was uncompromising. For him Islam was above everything else. While criticizing the existing order, Khomeini extolled the merits of an Islamic government, without specifying the mechanism by which it might be achieved. But he was bold enough to urge youngsters "to silence those who were criticizing the clergy publicly". Khomeini's views, however, were not shared by all mullahs.

The emergence of radio and newspapers, which fulfilled part of the social role of the pulpit, must have been an element in Khomeini's thinking. The clergy, to begin with, were unable to cope with a modern situation in which issues such as taxation and military conscription had to be answered. Instead of trying to find a religious justification, they opted for the easy way by rejecting them. Answering fundamental questions was no easy task, and many clergymen remained on the defensive.

Khomeini's attack against the anticlerical right came at a time when the threat of the left had not been felt fully by the Qom clergy. By the late 1940s, it was the rise of the communist party which sent shivers through the clerical spine. Another clergyman and a teacher of philosophy in Qom, Allameh Tabataba'i, with the help of Mortaza Motahhari, a student of Khomeini, spent several years studying Western philosophy in order to come up with a cohesive and logical response to materialism and Marxist ideas which had captured the imagination of the young people and increased the membership of the Tudeh Party.

While Khomeini and Tabataba'i confined themselves to religious centres, there were others directly in touch with the reality of life, and the requirements of the people. Among them were Ayatollah Mahmud Taleqani, a liberal clergyman, and Mehdi Bazargan, an engineering professor at Tehran University. Bazargan, who had to deal with young inquisitive minds in a scientific manner, embarked on presenting Islam as a religion compatible with science. At the same time Taleqani, aware of the impact of Marxism on young people, did some research on the nature of ownership and its limits in Islam, a question which still divides not only the clerical leadership in Iran but most Moslems.

While Khomeini was engaged in teaching, Ayatollah Kashani, a senior clergyman who later became parliamentary speaker, offered a political Islamic response. He supported the *Fedayeen-e Islam*, the Iranian version of Egypt's Moslem Brotherhood, led by Navvab Safavi. Safavi and Kashani appealed to the young clergy in the 1940s and, while Khomeini was in sympathy with both, he never engaged in political activity, fearing he would undermine his future. In part this was a reflection of the fact that the most prominent clergyman of the day. Ayatollah Borujerdi (d. 1960), discouraged political activity in religious centres.

Ayatollah Taleqani and Bazargan, who later formed the Freedom Movement of Iran in the 1950s, were gaining political influence at the expense of those clergy who either supported the Shah or remained neutral during the 1953 *coup d'état* which toppled the Mossadeq government. Taleqani and Bazargan tried, and to a certain extent succeeded, in attracting young people to religion by presenting it in a modern and progressive light. They even came to be influential among the young clergy. Following the death of Ayatollah Borujerdi, they published essays by leading theologians suggesting that the clergy should reform their way of thinking. Political events, however, took over from intellectual arguments and while the religious scene was in disarray, the Shah in 1962 introduced his "White Revolution" in order to undermine the religious establishment and take the initiative back from the left and nationalist opposition.

For two years the Shah dealt ruthlessly with his opponents, the most implacable of whom was the very Khomeini who had been more into scholarship and mysticism than political activity.

During 1962–64, Khomeini dared challenge the Shah's autocracy, his reforms, and his links with the United States but failed to undermine the regime. He did succeed, however, in establishing himself as the undisputed leader of the opposition. Khomeini's arrest and exile to Turkey in November 1964 and to Iraq a year later, gave him a free hand to break with the monarchy and the Shah altogether.

It was in the absence of Khomeini that Iranian society went through major transformations, both materially and intellectually. The Shah's reforms, though helping women to participate in the political and social life of the country, did not achieve the desired effect, but rather helped bring about social change and set in train the events which were eventually to lead to his downfall.

The Mullahs began to explain to the people that they were not against modern technology and science. To reject the accusations of being reactionary, the clergy began to learn about the outside world and modern disciplines. This enabled them to communicate with the young people whose attraction to the Shah's programmes was short lived. It was in this period that people like Ayatollah Beheshti, Ayatollah Motahhari, Dr Muhammad Javad Bahonar, Dr Muhammad Mofatteh and others, all of whom came to prominence after the revolution, played a major role.

Culturally, they attempted to introduce a new concept of Islam quite different from the traditional image. They began to establish private modern schools to teach an Islam which, they argued, was socially caring and politically compatible with freedom and progress. Although they were not always successful in converting the youth to their cause, they contributed to a weakening of faith in the Shah's secular reforms. As young people were being absorbed by left-wing guerrilla groups in large numbers, the Shah's regime had no alternative but to tolerate the preachers of dynamic Islam. Politically they established a semi-clandestine network of merchants and clergy loyal to Khomeini—a network which organized the Islamic revolution and took over once the Shah's regime began to disintegrate.

From the late 1960s and early 1970s, the religious, and to a certain extent intellectual, scene was dominated by one man: Ali Shari'ati. A French-educated sociologist, Shari'ati's writings and speeches captured the imagination of young students and attracted a whole generation of boys and girls to radical Islam. His influence was strongest on the issue of social justice in Islam, re-interpreting the history of Islam in general and Shi'ism in particular.

Following Shari'ati's death at the age of 44 in 1977, many of his followers formed the effective vanguard of the revolution and played an influential role after the Islamic regime came to power. Shari'ati, ironically, was criticizing a supposedly modern society which was suffering from materialism, alienation, and outdated values imposed on it in the name of religion.

The historic moment for the Islamic movement, at least theoretically, came in 1969 when Khomeini developed his thoughts on the concept of Islamic government in a series of lectures in the holy city of Najaf in Iraq. He eventually established this concept in 1979. Khomeini's concept of Islamic government is that, in the absence of the Prophet and his righteous successors, the Imams, it is the duty of religious leaders (*faqi*) to implement the divine law by forming an Islamic administration. In itself a controversial issue, it was largely Khomeini's sheer charisma and personality which ensured that it was taken seriously.

However, without the groundwork done by Khomeini's students and Islamicists such as Shari'ati, Taleqani and Bazargan, the idea of an Islamic government would not have had any appeal. In fact, the main body of the conservative clergy did their best to undermine Khomeini's theory. during the 1970's, supporters of the conservative clergy in Najaf destroyed copies of Khomeini's book.

Khomeini, and for that matter all other opposition groups, were taken by surprise by the swiftness of the revolution. They had not expected it to come so soon, and many theoretical arguments still remained unsettled when the Shah fell in 1979. So as not to play into the enemy's hand, the Islamicists had restrained themselves before the revolution. Nevertheless there were occasional bitter clashes between supporters of the various strands of thought. The competition for influence continued to be played out after the revolution.

ISLAM AFTER THE REVOLUTION

When the revolution succeeded, it was Ayatollah Khomeini who laid down the guidance for the "right" Islamic path. But he was not the only one. As a shrewd politician, Khomeini only gave general guidance, leaving others to interpret his words in the light of circumstances. Khomeini's priorities were to maintain and consolidate Islamic rule; to prevent the revolution from falling into the hands of anticlerical forces, as happened in the Constitutional Revolution; to create an Islamic society under his theory of "the guardianship of the juristconsult"; and finally to graft his blueprint of an Islamic society on to a state as envisaged by the Prophet Mohammed in the seventh century.

To achieve these objectives, Khomeini's approach was generally gradualist. While excluding the secular forces who hoped to wrest the leadership from the "simple minded mullahs", Khomeini included liberal Moslems like Bazargan and his supporters in the government. He then encouraged Islamic militancy among Shari'ati's followers who regarded Khomeini's anti-American stance as evidence of his firm belief in social justice and thereby helped him undermine the left.

Khomeini, however, was well aware that eventually he would have to choose between his clerical and secular supporters. He opted for the first. However, the main problem facing Khomeini then and now was the lack of a blueprint for an Islamic economy. Economic policy more than anything else has divided the clergy. The holy Koran and tradition of the Prophet are, to say the least, very vague. Islam can be seen as an ocean yielding all sorts of fish. Merchants, socialists, and economists have all found literature within Islam to support their cases. The divided Iranian clergy are no exception.

Since political questions were for the most part determined by Khomeini as the country's supreme leader, the clerical divisions show themselves more on economic and social issues. Some mullahs are in favour of radical change, others are reformists, but the majority, who have always resisted change, can be described as traditionalist. They include the senior Ayatollahs and most mullahs residing in theological centres. The three Grand Ayatollahs, Kho'i, who lives in Najaf, and Golpaygani and Marashi, of Qom, are the leaders of the traditionalists. They are not interested in politics, nor to begin with were they receptive to the concept of Khomeini's Islamic government. When they accepted the Islamic Republic as a political reality, they changed tack and used their influence to thwart the radicals on the question of social and economic reforms. They are strongly represented in the judiciary and in the Council of Guardians. Politically they are moderate and are often critical of the government stance on foreign policy and trade. Leading conservatives who have worked within the system include Ayatollah Azari-Qomi, who publishes the daily *Resalat* newspaper, Ayatollah Muhammad Yazdi and Ayatollah Mahdavi-Kani, former Prime Minister and a close adviser of Ayatollah Khomeini.

At the other end of the political spectrum are the radicals. They are the young turks of Islam grouped together in a coalition of different movements. Politically loyal to the Ayatollah, their ideological background comes from a variety of sources: scientific justification of Islam, third world anti-americanism and Islamic socialism. They are strong among the student bodies, the younger generation of mullahs and the revolutionary organizations including the Revolutionary Guards. The radicals' theological base is very weak. They often justify their action through selective verses of the holy Koran, the tradition of the Prophet and some of the sayings of Ayatollah Khomeini.

They number among some of their more powerful figures, Hojatolislam Ali-Akbar Mohtashemi, Minister of Interior, and formerly ambassador to Damascus, who is known to have strong links with the *Hezbollah* in Lebanon; Hadi Ghaffari, the unofficial leader of those hard-liners who, in the name of *Hezbollah*, often attack their enemies with the benefit of close links with the security organizations; and Hojatolislam Muhammad Mussavi Khoiniha, the State Prosecutor, who is close to Ayatollah Khomeini, extremely articulate and shrewd.

The animosity between the traditionalists and the radicals is well illustrated in the strong views expressed in newspapers such as *Resalat* and *Keyhan*. What prevents a major break between them is the reformist faction, which includes the majority of leading personalities of the Islamic Republic, notably Ayatollah Meshkini, the Friday prayer-leader in Qom and the chairman of the Assembly of Experts, Hojatolislam Rafsanjani, Speaker of the *Majlis*, Commander-in-Chief and the only personality who has some form of link with most of Iran's power centres, and President Ali Khamenei.

While the radicals would like to abandon the traditional aspects of Islam as represented by the traditionalists, the reformists would like to change them. For instance, while the radicals were broadcasting music on the radio and television against the traditionalist wishes, it was Khomeini who stepped in and redefined pre-revolutionary edicts by decreeing that "if the music does not lead you towards sin but rather to elevated, revolutionary and Islamic sentiments then it is not forbidden". Khomeini has always guarded against any disunity among the clergy, knowing full well the political cost of such a schism.

The aspirations and ambitions of these factions and personalities have rendered the Islamic Constitution, drafted hastily after the revolution, unworkable even in Ayatollah Khomeini's lifetime. The Constitution is a mixture of Khomeini's theories on the one hand and a Western view of the separation of the three branches of power on the other. But in reality the institutions created in Islamic Iran are, in terms of power-politics, very different from those envisaged in the Constitution.

The most powerful institution is the Expediency Council, created only last year to arbitrate between the *Majlis* and the Council of Guardians. Khomeini's relative inactivity in his old age has enabled the Expediency Council to acquire enormous importance. Among its six "political" members, it includes Rafsanjani, Khamenei, Khoiniha and Prime Minister Moussavi.

Ahmad Khomeini sits as a non-voting member and there are six theologian members of the Council of Guardians. It effectively dominates five other key centres of power:

(i) The Assembly of Experts, the 83-strong body of theologians, with Ayatollah Meshkini at its head and Rafsanjani as his deputy, is in theory the most important institution in the land, with the power of appointing, advising and, if need be, dismissing the Leader/s.

(ii) The *Majlis-e Shura*, with 270 deputies of whom 150 are economic radicals.

(iii) General Command Headquarters. This newly-formed body is headed by Rafsanjani and is in charge of the Army, the Revolutionary Guards, the Bassij Volunteers, and the Gendarmerie.

(iv) The Ministry of Interior, headed by Hojatolislam Mohtashemi, a leading radical, who is also in charge of the Police, the Revolutionary Committees, and provincial governors.

(v) The Secretariat of Friday Prayer Leaders. This plays a major role in forming public opinion since the prayer leaders are the personal representatives of Ayatollah Khomeini. The majority are closer to the moderates and are under the guiding influence of Ayatollah Meshkini, Ahmad Khomeini, and Rafsanjani.

With such a complicated system of government, the Islamic Republic has yet to prove that Islam can provide an answer to the needs of contemporary society. In practice, the setbacks in the Gulf War and acceptance of the ceasefire have added fuel to a campaign to amend the constitution so as to give the President greater executive power.

The confusion in decision-making and the resultant chaos has cost Iran a great deal. A confused foreign policy led to its isolation from the international community. The main beneficiaries of this erratic behaviour were Iran's enemies, notably Iraq. Even those Moslem organizations and parties throughout the Islamic world which had hailed the revolution enthusiastically began to distance themselves from Iran's record on human rights. This left Iran with radical supporters such as *Hezbollah* in Lebanon, whose identification with hostage-taking is universally recognized. Support for *Hezbollah* among the leadership's radical wing is an embarrassment to the moderates.

The cost of the war, the fall in oil prices, and lack of economic direction have led to more poverty. The secular-minded educated women have been forced out of most official positions, leaving little opportunities outside their homes except for jobs such as nursing and teaching. On the other hand, the village schools are now for the first time full of girls. The villagers have no reservation in sending their children to the school now that they consider it to be run on Islamic principles. In general, villagers have more access to the main towns and are closer to the government, although they feel free to criticize it through the ballot box. The arrival of public telephone and television has ensured the regimes' hold over the rural areas. Every Friday the village clergyman will tell the villagers more or less what Rafsanjani has told the Tehranis in person, interpreting the latest shift in the political situation with regard to war and peace, foreign policy, economy, and religious issues.

To some extent, the villagers see that, as a result of the revolution, some of their values and norms have been imposed, at least superficially, on the urban centres of the country. But deep down the Westernization that existed in Iran before 1979 is now creeping into the village life through the revolution itself. Village girls who can afford to do so now wear Western style dresses under the chador. The village, perhaps for the first time, is a microcosm of Iran. The issues concerning villagers, such as land tenure and water supplies, as well as those related to urban people, such as trade and employment, are a major problem for the Islamic regime.

For those who have given everything, including their beloved sons, for the war and the revolution, the least they expect from the Islamic regime is a minimum decent standard of life. In the past ten years the shortcomings of the regime have been attributed to the post-revolutionary chaos and to the war. These can no longer be used as excuses, however, and as the period of reconstruction begins, the Islamic Republic is under the spotlight before its own people.

Its first decade could perhaps be analysed objectively only from a perspective free of revolutionary chaos, war, and internal unrest. We may witness the first two prerequisites soon, but the third may take a little longer. If we agree with the general view that Rafsanjani is the post-Khomeini leader of Iran, then the reconstruction policy will make or break him. Rafsanjani will have to move quickly to meet some of the basic economic demands of a disappointed and disgruntled population, some of whom look back nostalgically to the Shah's time. Ten years of revolution and nearly eight years of war have left behind a shattered, unproductive economy. A third of the work force is out of work or engaged in the military, although on the positive side Iran is free from the problems of foreign debt.

The slogans of the revolution ten years ago were: *"Azadi, Esteqlal, Jumhori-ye Eslami"* (Freedom, Independence, Islamic Republic). None of these aspirations have been fully realized. Whatever happens to the revolution and the present regime, the Ayatollah has started the process of reform in Islam. If the regime succeeds in adapting Islam to respond to contemporary requirements, it will be the beginning of an Islamic reformation. Otherwise the way could be paved for a genuine secular movement to emerge out of the people's experience: an experience that would be durable since it would not be imposed from above as the Shah tried to do.

A key figure in the Iranian religious scene, Ayatollah Mortaza Motahhari, who was a learned and an enlightened man, related an interesting story about the role of the mullahs in society. "I was talking to a group of seminarians in a theological school in Tehran", said Motahhari. "I told them the clergy's role in society should be similar to a driver. We should look right, we should look left, and then accelerate. We should avoid being mullah-brakes all the time. At this point", said Motahhari, "a seminarian commented wryly: we are not even mullah-brakes! We are mullah reverse-gears." Motahhari, who was assassinated after the revolution, worked hard to push the clergy forward and to change their image among the population in general. In the wake of the ceasefire, Khomeini has been trying to do the same. It may prove to be too late.

2. THE VIEW TO THE WEST: IRAN AND WESTERN EUROPE

Sir Anthony Parsons

Over four centuries the states of Western Europe had become accustomed to dealing with the Persian Empire: the ruling dynasties had changed from Safavid to Zand to Qajar to Pahlavi, but the structure of kingship provided the continuity. Shah Mohammed Reza Pahlavi's celebration of 2,500 years of uninterrupted monarchy in 1971 may have been an exercise in hyperbolic bombast but, in contemporary terms, Iran seemed likely to European observers to provide an exception to the twentieth-century Asian and African experience that, sooner or later, kings must give way to republican-minded colonels or radical politicians. By the mid-1970s, the Shah had become part of the regional, indeed the global, landscape: he had reigned and ruled for over 30 years. The Kings of Egypt, Libya, Iraq and Afghanistan had gone, while the Pahlavi Court, with its aura of success and wealth, had become a magnet for deposed European monarchs: the former Kings of Greece, Italy and Albania were among the frequent royal visitors.

Moreover, Pahlavi Iran had assumed increasing importance to Western Europe during the decades following the end of the Second World War. While Arab states used their oil exports as a political weapon in the Arab-Israeli wars of 1956, 1967 and 1973, Iranian oil exports were never used as such. The oil nationalization crisis in 1951 had led to an apparently stable relationship between Iran and an Anglo/Dutch/American consortium. With the ending of British protection of the Arab states of the southern Gulf in 1971, Iran had, with Saudi Arabia, become a key player in the maintenance of regional stability and of the free flow of oil through the Strait of Hormuz.

Admittedly, in the turbulent aftermath of the 1973 war, the Shah had been primarily responsible for the threefold increase in the price of OPEC crude oil with all that this meant in terms of disruption of international finance and consequent recession and inflation. But the massive wealth accruing to Iran as a result had transformed the country into a highly lucrative export market and source of investment finance. Iran provided substantial loans to Britain and France and invested in West German industry. European industrialists, businessmen and merchant bankers poured into Tehran in search of the vast contracts arising out of the doubling of Iran's long-term spending in the five year plan announced in 1974, and the Shah's determination to make Iran the Japan of the Middle East—the drive to be characterized as the Great Civilization. And let it not be forgotten that it was the OPEC price hike which made economical the exploitation of British and Norwegian North Sea deposits. With a posted price below US$7 a barrel, North Sea development was not cost effective.

Quite apart from its enhanced importance from the commercial and financial points of view, Iran had, by 1978, assumed wider significance for Western European foreign policy interests. The Shah was using his country's wealth and influence to promote objectives which were complementary to those of the European Community—a "moderate" Arab approach to the Palestine problem, independence for Namibia, economic development in non-Marxist sub-Saharan Africa, Afghanistan and the Indian sub-continent.

With the Soviet Union active in Angola, Mozambique and the Horn of Africa, a communist takeover in Afghanistan in 1978 and continued tension in the Middle East, Iran came to be regarded as a weighty regional buttress to overall Western interests. In a nutshell, Pahlavi Iran in the Shah's last years was more attractive materially and more important politically to Western Europe than at any previous period of modern history, with the possible exception of the Second World War following the German invasion of the Soviet Union.

In 1978–79, the utterly unexpected happened. The apparently impregnable monarchy, supported by a loyal officer corps and a pervasive secret police force, was brought down by cumulative popular protest, giving birth to a regime which was in all respects the antithesis of Pahlavism. Republican austerity replaced imperial ostentation; America's second closest ally in the region became her sternest adversary; a fierce independence of foreign entanglements replaced a growing network of overseas connections; and social and cultural Westernization gave way to fundamentalist Shia Islam. "Death to the Shah. Neither West nor East. Only the Islamic Republic." This slogan of the revolution said it all.

The member states of the European Community have spent the past 10 years trying to come to terms with this phenomenon and to protect their interests as best they can in the profoundly changed circumstances. This chapter is an attempt to draw up a balance sheet of their success and failure with special reference to Britain, France, West Germany and Italy.

BILATERAL RELATIONS

Of the four leading EC countries the **UK** was the most dangerously exposed to hostile reaction from the revolutionaries. Since 1953, the United States, previously regarded by Iranians as a potential St George pitted against the dragon of British imperialism, had itself become the super-dragon of Iranian popular sentiment. America was seen as the destroyer of the nationalist hero, Dr Mohammed Mossadeq, the principal abettor of an "illegitimate" Shah, the corruptor, through the permeation of mass Western culture, of the Iranian/Islamic tradition, and the overwhelming presence which Iran must shake off in order to be truly independent: in a phrase "the Great Satan".

However, Iranian folk memory is long and Britain was still, to use Ayatollah Khomeini's colourful characterization, "the aged wolf of imperialism". Britain (and Tsarist Russia) had dominated Iran from the early nineteenth century until 1918, and Britain had carried on with the good work when the 1917 Revolution removed Russia from the imperial stage. Britain had monopolized Iranian oil for half a century (until Dr Mossadeq nationalized the Anglo-Iranian Oil Company in 1951) and, as Iranians saw it, had exploited their country's natural wealth to its own advantage. In Iranian mythology, Britain had been behind Reza Shah's seizure of power in the 1920s. Britain (aided by the Soviet Union) had invaded Iran in 1941 and had put Reza Shah's son on the throne. The UK's might had declined in relation to that of the United States but the hidden British hand was still everywhere: Britain's scheming had manipulated the American Juggernaut which had crushed Mossadeq. Britain was the Shah's partner in the Central Treaty Organisation (Cento) which debarred Iran from her natural place in the Non-Aligned Movement. Britain, once the leader, was now second only to America in the popular Iranian demonology, the Soviet Union occupying a different, although equally disagreeable area of the Inferno. In the year of the revolution it became abundantly clear to me that all our efforts over the previous quarter century to bury the past and construct a normal relationship with Iran, free of paranoia and neuroses, had yet to bear fruit. From the Shah himself downwards, within the regime and amongst the opposition, the legend was ineradicable. The British leopard could not have changed her spots. If you were clever enough you could always trace a British motive and British plotting behind all events, even those destructive of Pahlavi rule, or indeed of British interest. When I left Tehran in January 1979 I did not anticipate that my successor as Ambassador would find it easy to establish a trouble-free relationship with the new leadership.

France was less exposed. Defeat in the Napoleonic Wars had eliminated her from the competition for political and military influence in Iran in the age of imperialism; as already mentioned, Britain and Tsarist Russia had scooped that pool. However, throughout the nineteenth century, French cultural influence, as in Egypt, grew without posing the "imperialist" threat of the British and later the American equivalents. By the beginning of the twentieth century, the Western-educated classes in Iran were Francophone rather than Anglophone: Iranian intellectual opponents of the Shah at the time of the constitutional crisis of the early 1900s were operating from Paris, rather than London or St Petersberg, and French political ideas were permeating Iranian intellectualism.

By the 1970's France had built a close relationship with the Shah and his Paris-educated Empress and with the Pahlavi establishment: French cultural and commercial interests were flourishing. But at the time of the revolution, the opposition was once again based in Paris. Harried by the authorities in his exile in southern Iraq, Ayatollah Khomeini flew to Paris where he was joined by leading Francophone supporters, notably Sadeq Qotbzadeh (later Foreign Minister, executed in 1981) and Abolhassan Bani-Sadr (later President, but forced to flee to Paris in 1981). The suburb of Neauphle le Château became the headquarters of the revolution from which the Ayatollah was free to issue his directives. Unlike the American and British Embassies, no attacks were made on the French Embassy in Tehran and France must have been hopeful that the revolution would leave her interests in Iran relatively unscathed.

West Germany had even less to worry about. Except for the brief period of intimacy between Reza Shah and the Nazi regime from the 1930s up to his enforced abdication in 1941, there was no history of special political or military relations between the two countries. In the post-Second World War period West Germany concentrated with great success on promoting her commercial and industrial interests, steering clear of political entanglements. By the time of the revolution, Germany was by far the largest European exporter of goods and services to the Iranian market and was in the process of constructing two nuclear power stations at Bushehr on the Persian Gulf. German technology had penetrated the traditional manufacturing sector of the urban bazaar and thousands of Iranian workers had been trained in German factories. The German cultural centre in Tehran (the Goethe Institute) had made itself available to oppositional literary figures. Germans in Iran were liked and respected without resentment.

Italy too had a promising commercial relationship with Iran. Italian engineers were active in dam building and an Italian firm was managing a huge urban development in southern Iran.

For some months in 1979 the revolution took a predictable course. Alongside the formal government headed by Mehdi Bazargan, which was trying to reconcile popular aspirations with domestic tranquillity and a realistic sense of national interest, an informal apparatus of power had come into existence, comprising the revolutionary committees (*nomitehs*) and the incipient Revolutionary Guard. It soon became clear that these ardent spirits, confident of the ultimate backing of Ayatollah Khomeini, were out of the control of the constituted authorities. The saga of the Anglican Church, long established in Isfahan and other cities, was a case in point. The Church was an obvious target, combining as it did an evangelical alternative to Islam and a historic connection in Iranian folklore with the British Embassy and the protection of the British government. In February 1979 the (Iranian) pastor at Shiraz was murdered. Between June and October the Christian hospitals in Shiraz and Isfahan and the Mission for the Blind were confiscated; the Bishop's House and diocesan offices in Isfahan were invaded and looted of documents and personal effects; the (Iranian) Bishop himself was interrogated by a revolutionary judge. In October, an attempt was made on the Bishop's life during which his courageous wife was wounded. In May 1980, a female British missionary was savagely attacked in Tehran and the Bishop's son was murdered. In August five missionaries including three British subjects (amongst them the woman who had been attacked) were arrested. The three Britons were released in February 1981 following the intercession of the Archbishop of Canterbury's envoy, Terry Waite. But all Anglican activities had by that time been proscribed. At all stages the authorities had shown sympathy with the Church's predicament but had been powerless to act.

Simultaneously, bilateral diplomatic relations between Britain and Iran declined to the lowest level ever, short of a formal breach. In August 1980 a major demonstration took place outside the American Embassy in London at which about 80 Iranians were arrested. Some went on hunger strike while other hunger striking demonstrators organized a "sit in" outside the British Embassy in Tehran. The British government wisely withdrew the Embassy staff in anticipation of their suffering a similar fate to that of their American colleagues. (At that time the American Embassy hostages had been held for nine months.) Sweden was asked to look after British interests, although the Iranian Embassy in London remained open. (Shortly before this development the Iranian Embassy had been invaded by dissidents of ethnic Arab origin. The siege was broken by British SAS commandos who stormed the building and released the Iranian staff.) From that time on, British interests were represented in Iran only by a small "Interests Section" under the Swedish flag. All British staff were again withdrawn in 1987 following a bizarre incident in which a British diplomat in Tehran was abducted and beaten in retaliation for the arrest of an Iranian consular official in Manchester on a charge of shoplifting. At the time of writing (October 1988) an agreement in principle has been reached to restore full diplomatic representation but, as is always the case with Iranians, monarchical or republican, the detailed negotiations are proving difficult and replete with pitfalls.

In the event the tranquillity of Franco-Iranian relations did not last. Paris again became the focal point for Iranian plotters, from radical republicans to liberal constitutionalists and extreme monarchists. The able and popular Prince Shahriyar Shafiq, son of Princess Ashraf, the Shah's twin sister, was assassinated in Paris in 1979, presumably by agents of the regime. In 1980 an attempt was made on the life of the Shah's last Prime Minister, Shapour Bakhtiar, in his Paris apartment. In 1984 Paris was the scene of the assassination of Gen. Oveissi, formerly Commander Land Forces and Martial Law Commander in 1978: Oveissi had also been in Baghdad shortly before the Iraqi invasion of Iran in September 1980.

In 1981, the wide spectrum of Paris-based conspirators was joined by ex-President Bani-Sadr, along with Massoud Rajavi and other leaders of the radical *Mujaheddin-e Khalq* who had been routed after fierce street battles in Tehran. They formed the "National Resistance Council for Liberty and Independence", with Rajavi at the head.

The presence in France of these dissident groups soured relations between Paris and Tehran. Bani-Sadr and his associates were granted political asylum on condition that they did not engage in political activity; an Iranian demand for extradition was refused. France's military aid to Iraq further lowered its standing in Iranian eyes. Anti-French demonstrations were staged in Tehran; there was a mutual withdrawal of ambassadors and French nationals were advised to leave Iran.

In the years to come, France's progressively pro-Iraqi stance kept relations with Tehran at a low ebb, compounding Iranian resentment at the Paris-based plotting. In 1984 a bomb exploded at Tehran Railway Station killing 18 people and injuring 300. The speaker of the Iranian parliament, Hojatolislam Rafsanjani blamed France for this outrage as the harbourer of "criminal leaders". Simultaneously an Air France air-craft was hijacked to Tehran; the hijackers demand for the release of those arrested for the attempt on Bakhtiar was not met and the incident ended peacefully.

In 1986, the new French Prime Minister, M. Jacques Chirac, set out to normalize relations with Iran, in the hope that Tehran would use its influence to bring about the release of two French journalists held hostage by Shia extremists in Beirut. A high level French delegation visit to Tehran had preceded this initiative. A French line of credit to Iran was opened and the journalists were freed. Iranian anger at the presence of opposition activists was assuaged by the expulsion from France in early 1987 of the *Mujaheddin* leaders (who then settled in Baghdad).

But the Franco-Iranian *rapprochement* was short-lived. In July 1987 the French judicial authorities wished to question an Iranian national named Vahit Gordji in connection with a series of murderous bomb outrages in France. Gordji claimed diplomatic immunity and took refuge in the Iranian Embassy. French police surrounded the building. The French Embassy in Tehran was reciprocally besieged and a charge of drug-smuggling and espionage was laid against a French diplomat. France severed diplomatic relations.

It was not until the run-up to the French presidential elections in 1988 that the imaginative diplomacy of M. Chirac (a candidate for the presidency) succeeded in mending all the outstanding fences. Gordji was allowed to leave France without being interrogated; the siege of the French Embassy was lifted; France repaid the large loan borrowed from the Shah for the (subsequently cancelled) nuclear power stations contract; and the remaining three French hostages in Beirut were released. Diplomatic relations were resumed.

West Germany and Italy have, as might have been expected, experienced a less stormy passage than Britain and France, and their commercial enterprises have continued to prosper. There have, however, been minor incidents.

In 1982 there were clashes between rival groups of Iranians at Mainz and seventeen were deported. Iran briefly closed its embassy and consulates. The following year, the former Deputy Foreign Minister, Sadeq Tabatabai (see passage on the hostage crisis below) was arrested at Düsseldorf for allegedly smuggling opium. He was released on bail a few weeks later and returned to Iran. The Italians had a brief row over the broadcast of a television programme derogatory to Khomeini, and in 1984, an Iran Air aircraft was hijacked to Rome, probably by the *Mujaheddin*. The hijackers surrendered.

Following this brief sketch of bilateral relations, it is appropriate to look at how the two sides—Western Europe and Iran—fared in the major events which dominated the first decade of the revolution in the eyes of the outside world, namely the hostage crisis and the Iran/Iraq war.

THE HOSTAGE CRISIS

If the Iranian leadership believed that the fourteen month crisis which began with the seizure of the American Embassy in Tehran in November 1979 could be isolated as an Irano/American dispute, they were quickly disillusioned. The UN Security Council was seized of the problem from the outset and the whole world—East, West and Non-Aligned—reacted with horror at the outrage. Europe was no exception. Britain and France, the two European Permanent Members, gave the United States full support in the Council and voted for the sanctions resolution sponsored by the United States in January 1980 (vetoed by the Soviet Union, most probably as a result of the bad blood between the super-powers arising out of reaction to the Soviet invasion of Afghanistan a few weeks earlier). Meanwhile West Germany, had already announced the suspension of credit guarantees to Iran. Britain had frozen all Government of Iran and Central Bank assets in London.

After the defeat of the sanctions resolution, the United States formally broke relations with Iran, applied an economic embargo and urged its European allies to do likewise. The European Community, to American annoyance, was reluctant to do so, not, as many people in the United States suspected, out of commercial greed: more because sanctions were regarded as probably counter-productive and conducive to strengthening the hands of the Iranian extremists, and because of fear that a Western embargo would deliver the Iranian economy into the hands of the Soviet Union and its Comecon partners. Support in the Security Council had been given out of loyalty to an ally in distress, not out of conviction that sanctions would accelerate the end of the crisis. In the event the European Community adopted a package of sanctions which was more symbolic than actual. The embargo on exports to Iran applied only to contracts concluded prior to Nov.4, 1979 (in the case of Britain only those concluded after June 1980). There was also dissent between the United States and the Community over the legitimacy of the freezing of Iranian assets in the European branches of American banks.

By the end of the summer of 1980, when war with Iraq was clearly threatening and the Iranian leadership was beginning to realize that there was nothing further to be gained from a prolongation of the hostage crisis, the fact that West Germany had maintained good relations with the new regime proved a valuable asset. The Iranian Deputy Foreign Minister, Sadeqh Tabatabai, made contact with the German ambassador in Tehran, whom he knew well, and sought his mediation to meet the American side. This was arranged through the auspices of Bonn and proved to be the first move in the process of negotiation which eventually led to the release of the hostages.

In retrospect, in spite of occasional American irritation with her allies, the United States can have had no cause for complaint at the solidarity shown by Europe. More important perhaps for the future, Tehran should have concluded that gross infringements of international behaviour were likely to be met with a monolithic response from the West and that there was no serious chance of dividing the United States from her partners—the bizarre and/or cynical behaviour of the United States and of certain European governments in regard to horse (or arms) trading for the release of hostages held by Iranian-backed Shia gangs in Beirut lay far in the future.

THE IRAN/IRAQ WAR.

When Iraq invaded Iran on Sept.22, 1980, the UN Security Council did not even meet for some days. Iraq had brought strong and successful pressure on the seven non-aligned members of the Council to oppose a meeting in order to avoid international interference in what President Saddam Hussein wrongly believed to be a short blitzkrieg. This belief was perhaps based on the advice of the same Iranians whose counsel had proved so disastrous to the Shah. None of the rest of the Council membership, including the Europeans, was disposed to override this obstacle. The continuing hostage crisis had alienated international opinion to the extent that no state was ready to come to Iran's defence. By the same token, the Europeans supported the first resolution (No 479 of Sept.28) which, while calling for a cessation of hostilities, did not demand Iraqi withdrawal from Iranian territory. Even after the hostage crisis ended in January 1981, the council maintained its pro-Iraqi bias.

By 1982 Iraq was very much on the defensive and clamorously ready for peace: Iran was perceived internationally as obstinately prolonging the war by insisting on her original war aims of "identifying and punishing the aggressor". The Europeans supported all the resolutions which called for withdrawal to internationally recognized frontiers when it was a question of Iran withdrawing from Iraqi occupied territory, and went along with the tendency of the Council to address its strictures to both sides even when it was clear that it had been Iraq which had, for example, initiated the "tanker war", air attacks on open cities and the use of poison gas (in only one statement by the President of the Council, in March 1986, was Iraq specifically named for the use of chemical weapons).

Interestingly, in 1987 and 1988, membership of the Council included all four of the European states under discussion, namely Britain and France (Permanent Members) as well as West Germany and Italy (non-Permanent Members). They were all active in the formulation of Resolution 598 on which the present peace talks were based.

Bilateral European attitudes towards the war differed somewhat from the solidarity demonstrated in the Security Council. From the outset Britain adopted a policy of strict neutrality, embargoing the export of all military equipment to both sides except for the ill-defined category of "non-lethal" items. This provision enabled Britain to export to Iran a large supply ship originally contracted to the Shah's government. The Iranian Purchasing Office (a main centre for the acquisition of weaponry on the international market) in London remained open until 1987. Britain also despatched a small force of warships (the Armilla Patrol) to the southern Gulf in 1980 to render assistance to British merchant shipping.

France, on the other hand, came down openly on the Iraqi side in 1981 with the supply of Mirage F1 aircraft (which Iran described as an act of war). Simultaneously, under strong Iranian pressure, France agreed to release to Iran three missile launching boats which had been ordered by the Shah (one of them was briefly hijacked in the Mediterranean by the former Commander-in-Chief of the Imperial Iranian Navy!) In 1983 the French Foreign Minister visited Baghdad and France subsequently loaned to Iraq five Super-Etendard aircraft armed with Exocet missiles. There is no doubt that these acquisitions made a significant difference to Iraq's capability, particularly in the "tanker war" against shipping and oil installations on the Iranian side of the Gulf. France, with the United States, was also one of the most vociferous advocates of a unilateral arms embargo against Iran when Tehran equivocated over resolution 598 (Britain was almost equally enthusiastic).

West Germany and Italy, with major interests in both camps, pursued a neutral policy throughout, although Italy joined other European governments—Britain, France, the Netherlands and Belgium—in sending warships to the Gulf in 1987 when the foreign armada gathered there to escort flagged shipping on the Arab side, thus inhibiting Iranian retaliation and giving greater impunity to the Iraqis to prosecute their campaign against Iranian shipping and oil installations.

When, on July 18, 1988, Iran, to the astonishment of the world and, I suspect, of its own people, announced its acceptance of Resolution 598, international opinion began to turn away from its long-held pro-Iraqi posture. The threat of an outright Iranian victory, with its profound consequences for the region as a whole, had disappeared and for a few weeks, Iraq appeared for the first time as the recalcitrant party. In particular, Iraqi use of chemical weapons against military and civilian targets, unequivocally stated in reports by a UN mission, excited strong censure and led to the adoption of a unanimous Security Council resolution (620) on Aug.26, 1988. This resolution, which was co-sponsored by West Germany, Italy, the UK and Japan (but not France) decided to consider appropriate measures should there be any further use of chemical weapons wherever and by whomever committed. It was followed on Sept.15 by an overwhelming vote of censure in the European parliament accusing Iraq of using chemical weapons in Kurdistan and calling on European Community governments to suspend the sale of arms and "chemical substances and equipment" to Iraq.

Hence, at the time of writing (late October 1988) Europe has returned to a more impartial position between Iran and Iraq and, with the recent negotiations between London and Tehran, all Community governments are now in, or about to be in, full diplomatic relations with Iran. The wheel has come close to full circle after ten years.

It is always perilous to attempt to gaze into the future, particularly where Iran is concerned. Apart from anything else, West Germany and Italy will shortly leave the Security Council on completion of their two-year terms as non-Permanent Members, thus weakening the Community voice in that forum which will have a crucial part to play in maintaining momentum in the peace negotiations, at present at a virtual standstill—but the cease-fire has now held for two months.

Provided that there is no recurrence of hostilities with Iraq and provided that there is no domestic upheaval in Iran which blows the leadership off its present course of mending fences with the outside world, abandoning attempts to export the revolution and concentrating on domestic consolidation and economic reconstruction, there is even reason to hope that relations between Iran and the Community will move into quieter waters with advantage to both sides. So long as the breach with the United States remains open, Europe will figure very largely in Iranian calculations.

But there are still problems to be solved. Europe expects Iran to use its undoubted influence to bring to an end the nightmare of the hostages held in Beirut. All the French and German hostages are now free but, apart from the Americans and others there are still three British hostages in captivity. Additionally two British subjects have been held prisoner in Tehran for over two years—nearly three in one case—without charge or trial. Accusations of espionage have been levelled at one of them. Until these questions have been satisfactorily resolved, I cannot envisage a fully normal relationship with Tehran. In broader terms, the revolution leadership must realise that adherence to the accepted norms of international behaviour is an essential precondition to the acceptance of Iran as a member in good standing of the international community. In these respects the ball is in Iran's court. In return Europe must recognize, as I believe it now does, that the revolution is a fact; there must be no backward glances over the shoulder or encouragement of plotters. Iranian affairs are for Iranians, not outsiders, to settle.

The fluctuations in the fortunes of material interests are a useful barometer of inter-state relations. Conventional wisdom insists that there is a major political ingredient in commercial relations between industrialized and Third World countries, in particular where the latter tend towards socialism or corporatism and the government has a major say in the award of large contracts. The oil-rich states of the Middle East are often cited as the prime examples of this theory.

There was certainly some truth in this notion in the days of the Shah. Although the majority of "bread-and-butter" trade in the private sector was done on the basis of commercial norms—prices, delivery dates, after sales service, etc.—there is no question that political (and other less reputable) factors entered into the award of public sector contracts—power stations, steel mills, nuclear reactors, military equipment, roads, railways, ports, etc. All other things being equal, a particular country could expect to benefit commercially from a close political relationship and vice versa. In this context it is useful to examine the performance of the six principal OECD countries (West Germany, Japan, France, Italy, Britain and the United States) over the decade since the revolution. The following is a comparative table showing the percentage of the Iranian import market held by each of these countries between 1978 and 1987:

	1978	1987
Germany	21.9	26.2
Japan	17.4	17.5
Italy	6.9	8.4
Britain	9.4	8.3
France	5.8	3.0
United States	23.9	0.9
Total	85.3	64.3

Certain interesting deductions can be drawn from this table. First, the fall in the share in the total market of the OECD Six has fallen (21%) almost exactly by the amount of the decline in the United States share (23%). Secondly, as I understand it the greater part of this gap has been filled by Turkey and Eastern European states such as Bulgaria and Yugoslavia which are conveniently situated to use the overland route to Iran

D

via Turkey. Thirdly, the European Community share has, notwithstanding the earthquake of the revolution, remained almost constant (44.0% in 1978; 45.9% in 1987). Fourthly, Britain's share, in spite of the virtual absence of diplomatic representation, has remained stable (Iran was still amongst Britain's top twenty markets in the developing world in 1986 and, in the Middle East, third only to Saudi Arabia and the United Arab Emirates).

Economists will tell me that it is facile to draw firm conclusions from such statistics. But the figures do suggest that even a violent and disruptive political event such as the Iranian revolution does not necessarily change traditional patterns of trade except in extreme circumstances such as the Irano/American breach with its attending embargoes, freezing of assets, etc. What will be really interesting will be the impact of the inevitable return to competition in the Iranian market of the United States, the absence of which led to a 23% gap, quickly filled by others.

3. THE VIEW TO THE WEST: IRAN AND THE UNITED STATES

Amit Roy

Sooner or later, Iran's relations with the United States—"the Great Satan" in Ayatollah Khomeini's colourful language—are likely to be mended. The reasons for this go beyond America's wish to keep a country as vitally strategic as Iran out of the Soviet Union's clutches, or Iran's need to ease its international isolation by making up with the United States.

These factors are important enough, but there is another more fundamental reason for believing that the divorce between Washington and Tehran is not permanent. There appears to be in the Iranian character an almost childlike desire to win approval from the West, in general, and America, in particular. Iran's middle-class intelligentsia, whose members remain pro-Western in temperament and were often American-educated in the past, has not been entirely neutralized by the revolution.

Of course, no one should under-estimate the obstacles to even the formal restoration of diplomatic relations, broken by President Carter in April 1980, following the seizure of hostages at the United States embassy.

Television coverage in the United States of the 444-day hostage crisis largely shaped American perception of Iran as a lawless land run by extremist clergymen. However, the dramatic footage sent back from Tehran by the networks of huge anti-American demonstrations often failed to penetrate the surface of a very complex relationship between the two countries.

For example, an almost daily ritual would occur outside the occupied embassy. The American television crews would arrive to film the large but usually good-humoured crowds outside the besieged embassy. But the moment the cameras were switched on, the crowds would explode into frenzied slogan-shouting and fist-waving: *"Marg bar Omrika!"* (Death to America).

The edited highlights, broadcast nightly on prime-time American news programmes, created the erroneous impression that all Iran was swimming in a sea of anti-United States hysteria.

What viewers did not see was that the moment the cameras were switched off, the crowds returned to normal behaviour. The curious would invariably step forward and happily chat with American journalists.

The point about the Iranian masses, especially outside Tehran, is they have only marginal influence on the formulation of policy. They are fickle, volatile and easily manipulated. The absence of personal animosity has been discovered by the few American journalists who have been given visas to visit Iran in recent years. They came with nameless fears but found ordinary Iranians remarkably amiable. Even Khomeini, who has blamed the United States for causing much of Iran's problems, drew a distinction between the American government and the American people.

In future, Iran is likely to seek a more balanced international trading relationship to avoid its previous mistake of becoming over-dependent on any one country. In the 1960s and 1970s, American armaments and technicians poured into Iran and a large part of the country's industrial and defence infrastructure was built with United States assistance. The West Germans have now replaced the United States as Iran's principal trading partner. But so numerous were the industrial links that bound Iran and America that they cannot all be severed as the country begins reconstruction after the costly eight-year war with Iraq.

Since 1979, Khomeini has laid down the broad outlines of policy, and anti-Americanism has been one of his central planks. It is unrealistic to expect that his deep-rooted hatred of the United States will soften. Having lived through the reign of both the late Shah, Mohammed Reza—who exiled him for 15 years—and that of his father, Reza Shah, Khomeini holds the Pahlavi dynasty responsible both for turning Iran into a virtual client state of the USA and for departing from orthodox Islam.

But who will determine Iran's stance towards the United States after Khomeini's death? Certainly not the Foreign Ministry, which traditionally has been one of the weakest government departments. Although the diplomats from the Shah's days have gone, the Ministry is still considered to be tainted with the pro-Western outlook of imperial times.

Some of Khomeini's principal lieutenants, notably Hojatolislam Rafsanjani, have revealed a willingness to deal with the United States when it has been in their interest to do so. This was apparent in 1986 when certain Iranian leaders, including Khomeini himself, showed they were prepared to barter American hostages (held by pro-Iranian *Hezbollah* groups in Lebanon) for weapons badly needed for the war against Iraq.

In the aftermath of Khomeini's death, there is inevitably going to be a period of instability as rival groups fight to establish their authority, Ayatollah Montazeri, who has been nominated Khomeini's spiritual successor but who has yet to prove he can hold on to the job, is not particularly pro-Western. He is also an advocate of exporting the revolution which has already inspired a fundamentalist, anti-American wave across the Moslem world.

Among other key clergymen, neither Hojatolislam Mohtashami, the Interior Minister, nor Hojatolisman Mohammed Khoiniha, the Prosecutor General, who played a leading role during the siege of the American Embassy, are likely to support closer ties with the United States.

It seems unlikely that anyone is going to risk his position during any power struggle by openly advocating improved relations with Washington. There are other obstacles. Iran is continuing to demand the return of its assets, worth billions of dollars, which were frozen by President Carter during the hostage crisis. Recent history is also not going to be helpful.

In the Gulf War, the United States tilted in Iraq's favour. The American armada in the Gulf sank or damaged Iranian vessels, some of which had probably sown mines in busy shipping lanes; bombed Iranian oil installations; and, by mistake, shot down an Iranian passenger aircraft with 290 people on board.

Another factor is that Iran has undergone critical demographic changes in the past decade. Its population has jumped dramatically from 33,000,000 in 1979 to nearly 50,000,000 ten years later. The young—and this includes the 400,000-strong revolutionary guards whose role in any power struggle will be crucial—have undoubtedly absorbed into their psychological make-up some of the anti-American propaganda to which Khomeini has exposed them.

However, it is by no means certain that the revolution has changed all important aspects of life. Although it has transformed the political structure of the country and given Islamic institutions a dominating role, it has failed to alter basic Iranian character or culture.

People still love to eat out, dance and listen to music (in private) and enjoy picnics with the family. The better-off dream of flying off to London and Los Angeles.

Even the clergy, who are often accused of trying to drag Iran back in time, hanker after sleek limousines and like to fill their homes with Western gadgets. Iranians, more so than most other people in the Middle East, have a strong *bazaari* instinct, an inborn drive to trade and a weakness for money. The West will see these as redeeming defects.

The revolution has brought much hardship and shortages, while petro-dollars, earned during the period of the Shah, however politically repressive, gave Iranians a taste for the good things of life. In the minds of ordinary folk, good things are associated with Western things, and Western things with American.

How Iran deals with the United States will depend partly on the American attitude to Iran, and, of course, vice versa. In a remark with racist undertones, Iranians were once dismissed by Richard Helms, the former CIA director and American ambassador in Tehran (1973–76), as basically "traders and rugmakers". He did not understand that what elevates Iranians is that their lust for luxury is cloaked in a culture much older and more sophisticated than anything America has to offer.

The symbol of Iran's relationship with the United States remains the sprawling embassy building which now stands empty, its gates locked, on Tehran's Taleghani Avenue. The crowds who demonstrated outside it have long since vanished along with the American television networks. The militant students dubbed it the "nest of spies" for it was from here that America maintained its special relationship with Iran.

The irony is that often the sound advice sent to Washington from its knowledgeable diplomats in Iran—for example, not to provoke a hostage crisis by allowing the exiled Shah to enter the United States in 1979—was ignored by politicians who thought they knew better.

The residents of Tehran still recall, with just a trace of nostalgia, the tall Christmas tree, decorated seasonally with fairy lights, peeping over the embassy walls. Even those who demonstrated outside the embassy would not be entirely displeased to see those lights burning again. For one thing, it would make applying for visas to visit "the Great Satan" so much easier.

4. THE POLITICAL BALANCE

Reza Navabpour

Despite the toil it exacted on Iranian life and the economy, the Gulf War was generally believed to be a "Heavenly Gift" enabling the survival of the Islamic regime in the face of foreign and domestic problems, including the tensions within the clerical leadership. Whether a "Heavenly Gift" or a "Heavenly Miracle", the war was at the same time a bosom to nourish as well as a forge to shape the Islamic regime, allowing it to grow amidst "tension" and to secure its continuity thanks to another quality in relations within the leadership—the element of "fusion".

From 1983 onwards, references to tension among Iran's rulers began to be made by Iranian leaders, including Hojatolislam Rafsanjani. Even earlier yet, soon after the establishment of the Islamic Republic, disagreements among the ruling clergy ("ulama") on a wide spectrum of social and economic issues, delayed or even halted some parliamentary decisions and the execution of certain government policies. The creation of a number of institutions, with parallel functions and, contradictory policies, and the occasional open clashes between them, is yet another indication of this tension. Following the end of the war, an attempt to abolish such institutions met with severe resistance. The closure of the Islamic Republic Party in 1987 and the leak of the American-Iranian contacts leading to the Irangate scandal, represent the peak of Iranian power politics prior to Iran's acceptance of UN Resolution 598, and the peaceful settlement of the war.

However, with the effective end of the war and the urgent need for a reconstruction programme, the deeply-rooted differences on social, political and economic issues, attained new dimensions. Against this background must be seen the execution of a number of clergy and politicians known for their sympathy for Ayatollah Montazeri, Ayatollah Khomeini's designated successor, as well as the mysterious murder of the politician Dr Kazem Sami,

Minister of Health in Dr Bazargan's provisional government. Dr Sami's name was being mentioned as a potential future prime minister. He too, was known for supporting Ayatollah Montazeri.

Foreign observers have frequently attempted to portray the leadership as being divided into two main rival groups, such as moderates v. radicals, conservatives v. reformists and left v. right on the basis of differences over foreign relations and/or economic issues. While these divisions certainly fuel internal tension, it is also necessary to recognize a counter-balancing element of "fusion", which helps hold the leadership together.

In a letter dated Oct.21, 1988, addressed to Ayatollah Khomeini, a leading member of his office, Hojatolislam Ansari Kermani, refers to "two ideological and political currents". He states that the serious differences between political personalities have confused him and many others. In his response printed in the Iranian press together with Ansari's plea, Khomeini refuses to accept that any fundamental issue is at stake, and refers to the differences as being merely differences of application—two different paths, leading to one and the same goal. Khomeini's advice for a "brotherly compromise", while seemingly simplistic, reflects the deep complexity of Iranian political composition, rather than any real division.

At first glance this response may seem like a balancing act on the part of Khomeini, contrary to his normal practice of utilizing his revolutionary might and charisma to denounce political groups or personalities that have, in his opinion, deviated from the path of revolution. A closer examination of Iranian political structure, however, would reveal the realities behind his cautious guidance. Ansari's letter, most probably prepared together with Khomeini's response, casts a light on the confusing nature of this structure. He observes a sharp polarity of views and interests on certain issues which contrasts with complete harmony and unity on other topics. A more confusing factor, in his view, is that most of the leading personalities of both factions are amongst Khomeini's disciples and associates and their rival institutions enjoy his support equally.

The complexity lies in a combination of the composite nature of leadership and the particular features of the Islamic revolution. An official promotional publication, printed abroad, refers to the Iranian revolution as a "divinely-inspired movement" in contrast to "other ordinary man-centred revolutions. . . . The main objective of the Islamic Revolution", accordingly, "has been, and continues to be, to rise up in fulfilment of Allah's injunctions regarding the protection of the secure sanctuary of Islam. . . . Contrary to the materialistic view that regards all things as stemming from material things and . . . puts mankind on a par with animals, Islam conceives of the entire universe as a manifestation of Allah's will". Hence the establishment of ecclesiastical regulatory institutions mainly, if not totally, controlled by the ulama, who see themselves, in contrast to secular leaders, as the only legitimate guardians of the Islamic community. They alone can ensure a consensus of religious belief and values and thereby fulfill the injunction of Allah.

In practice, however, the guardians of Allah's injunction have served a long apprenticeship in seeing their static ideologies at variance with the requisites of late twentieth-century social dynamics. In the last two centuries, the clergy have played an active role in Iranian politics. Their part in the Iranian Constitutional Revolution of 1905–1909 was of particular significance. Conversely, during the Pahlavi period (1925–1979), they lost most of their power and were at best a counter-balance, and throughout most of this period they followed a policy of quiescence. With the establishment of the Islamic Republic, however, it was not easy for them to find a unanimously acceptable policy spanning the division between the literal word of the scripture and the realities of modern politics. But with a great reserve of jurisprudential guardianship at their disposal, the grand Shia ulama are in a position to preserve the Islamic practices while keeping in step with the requirements of the time, and thereby exert their influence, not only on religious matters, but also on political, social and economic issues at large. It has been on this basis that Khomeini has been able to lay the foundations of a particular type of Islamic state in conformity with modern politics.

This is a departure from the origins of Islam, whose adherents maintain that it is a religion for all mankind, at all times and any amendments to the contents of the Koran and the deeds and sayings of the prophet Mohammad and the Imams are heretical. Some of the clergy, for instance, disagree with Khomeini's religious leniency and argue that, at least in certain areas, the Islamic Republic's modernist policies do not accord with Islamic law.

It is on the thin dividing line between these two extremes that the Islamic Republic's politicians find themselves. Whereas a few are at the polar points, presenting a relatively clear line of division, many others offer a confusing picture. This confusion is due to the absence of a clear definition of their aims and a lack of clarity in their ideas about basic social questions, for example the role of capital, landownership, state control of the economy, the degree to which the ulama are involved in politics, etc. These are issues which were the subject of debate long before the revolution.

In these circumstances, it is not rare to see individuals simultaneously supporting both factions on different issues. In fact the failure of the two factions to establish political parties and to draw up a definite programme on social, political and economic issues is far from being accidental. Some

E

institutions, newspapers and periodicals, as well as some of the political élite, have been known to take sides with one or other faction. Indeed some of these individuals and institutions are mentioned in Ansari's letter as representing two polar tendencies. Other observers have divided leading politicians and institutions into "statist" or "anti-statist" tendencies. But even these examples are not definitive. Some leaders seem to oscillate between the two and refrain from committing themselves to a defined social, political and economic viewpoint. For some, oscillation may well be a deliberate policy, where status and power depend more on the personal ability to manipulate political and public opinion, economic strings and foreign relations, than on any institutional basis. Political manoeuvrability is thus a key to political promotion in the hands of a skilful member of the ulama. In so doing, he would perpetuate, consciously or not, the state of political integration and provide the grounds for the element of "fusion" to coexist with "tension".

It is only in the context of such complexities that the striving for power within the leadership can be explained. While from a distance a division of tendencies is plain for all to see, too close a parallel with Western political dichotomies must not be drawn. What is fundamental to a westerner in shaping his society, such as economy, trade, property and landownership, is suggested by Khomeini to be subordinate to Islamic ideology and therefore of no grave significance. This allows Khomeini to intervene between the two factions without apparently committing himself to one or other tendency. Admittedly, since the end of the war, Khomeini has been less successful in retaining his impartiality. In spite of what Ansari suggests in his letter, Khomeini has increasingly given his support more evidently to Hojatolislam Rafsanjani and Prime Minister Moussavi. Rafsanjani further ascended the ladder of power by attaining the position of acting commander of the armed forces, and in spite of Ayatollah Montazeri's suggestive remarks that this is a full-time job, he managed to retain his office of the Speaker of parliament too.

The two factions found Khomeini's advice of brotherly relations crucial to the continuity of the Islamic Republic. Politically, however, both factions tried to manipulate Khomeini's mandate, as usual, for their own ends. President Khamenei, for instance, suggests that the differences are merely political. But he maintains that they concern the ruling establishment alone with the people having no share or interest in these differences. Following suit on Khomeini, he states that the presence of these differences, including those over economic issues, is a normal state of affairs with a long tradition and, seen from certain points of view, is in fact constructive too. At the same time he warns that an Islamic system is threatened not only by foreign powers but also internally by certain social groups—which he refrains from naming.

President Khamenei's avoidance of a direct attack fits well into the general pattern of counterbalance and explains its potential for continuity even under internal tension. The Iranian press testifies to the coexistence of warring politicians in parliament, the religious and governmental institutions and the cabinet. While cautious not to make direct accusations, the sympathizers of the two factions warn their audience of the growth of American or/and Russian brands of Islam. The Minister of Information, Hojatolislam Reyshahri, refers to the class mentality of a group of politicians whose ideas, in his opinion, are similar to Marxist ideology, and suggests that it is a Russian brand of Islam in disguise, which aims at defeating true Islam. By comparison, he maintains that the American brand of Islam is also a hostile development which is trying to separate religion from politics. Whereas the former is seemingly more dangerous to Islam as such, the latter is more of a threat to Islamic states. Like President Khamenei, Reyshahri too abstains from direct accusations. But it is not difficult to see what factions he is referring to with these two brands of Islam. What is important, however, is that by so threatening both extremes, like other Islamic leaders, he attempts to find a meeting point.

Reyshahri's apparent impartiality is neither accidental nor unique. It accords, for one thing, with the Islamic regime's slogan of "Neither West Nor East", and the "Pure Mohammedan Islam" referred to by Ayatollah Khomeini and other leaders of the Islamic Republic. However, once again it bears witness to the balance of power as well as to tension and fusion within the clerical leadership. His remarks, and similar comments by other ulama and politicians are evidence of the ideological split in the ranks of the ulama and the revival of a growing concern for an Islamic and just society, often compared with socialism, to replace the Shia nationalism prevailing during the Gulf War. It is interesting to note that the Gulf War, involving two Moslem nations, highlighted the notion of Iranian integrity as a "nation" rather than the Islamic "umma". The opposition of some of the ulama to the war was based on the idea that it posed a threat to the concept of Islamic unity and to the export of the revolution. It is erroneous, in their opinion, to refer to it as the Gulf War or the Iran-Iraq war; it was a unilaterally-imposed war brought about by American meddling. In practice some of the ulama and their adherents would have been pleased to see American military involvement. Ironically, however, the end of the war, failing to achieve its Islamic objectives and coming at a time when Iranians had suffered defeat, was a blow to the idea of Islamic unity, to the export of revolutionary ideas and consequently to the power of those ulama who supported these aims, notably Ayatollah Montazeri.

In the absence of a hostile foreign enemy, the anti-American propaganda machine seems to have lost its previous nationwide mobilizing force. Steps are already being taken towards commercial and political rapprochment with the West, including Britain. There are even indications for the eventual restoration of relations with the USA. The anti-Russian slogans, on the other hand, have never aroused a similar nationwide antagonism, and with the Russian withdrawal from the neighbouring Moslem country of Afghanistan and the modification of their domestic and international policies, they do not provoke outspoken hostility anymore. Thus, with other unifying focal points exhausted and the post-war social and economic problems pressing, the call for removal of class differences is bound to be attractive, especially as, in its concept of a just society, Islam correlates better with socialism than with all other twentieth-century ideologies. This is a change of national attitude reminiscent of the emergence of the Socialist Union in Egypt in the 1960s, which replaced the National Union of the 1950s following the collapse of Nasser's policy of union with Syria.

After his offer of resignation in early September, 1988, Moussavi once again acquired Khomeini's support, and continued to follow his policy for a planned economy, controlled by the government and operated mainly by co-operatives, leaving a limited role for the private sector. With such a policy, he stated in an interview, the revolution may be saved from running out of steam and giving in to the "American brand" of Islam.

Whatever its practicality, this is a language that appeals to the bulk of the deprived population in the post-war ideological vacuum, when the revolutionary symbols, particularly in the field of foreign politics, have lost much of their stimulating power. At the same time, some influential religious leaders and *Majlis* deputies, representing the interests of the private sector and large property owners, have formed a strong opposition. In the letter addressed to Prime Minister Moussavi, apparently covertly circulated in Iran and printed abroad, Ayatollah Montazeri voiced the feelings of those opposed to the government's policy of centralization and to tight control over trade. He states that even the socialist countries have come to their senses and adopted the open-door policy.

It is, however, not intended to associate Prime Minister Moussavi and Ayatollah Montazeri with two contradictory tendencies. As regards his other deeds and words, Ayatollah Montazeri is clearly concerned with the livelihood of low-income groups, and seemingly advocates greater state intervention. It is the government's policies, rather than principles, that he criticizes. Meanwhile, Moussavi's economic policies may well undergo gradual change as the threat of post-war civil disturbance recedes. The government's reluctance to take out foreign bank loans is an issue already open to question. Whereas adequate foreign exchange seems to be available to enable the government to continue financing the projects launched before the end of the war, the post-war reconstruction programmes call for extra funds to be supplied either by foreign bank loans, or the private sector. The government has, ironically, failed to improve its financial position with the end of the war—on the contrary the military budget has actually increased.

It would be almost suicidal for the government to succumb to the persuasive pressures exerted by foreign firms and financing sources and adopt an open-door policy. In addition to the disturbing effect this would have on the country's internal economic situation, the government shuns it because of its political and ideological repercussions.

Therefore, in order not to distance itself from the ideals of the revolution, the government has to rely upon internal sources. Here the dilemma is between the introduction of a rapid and major construction programme, which is likely to force the government to yield, at least to some extent, to the conditions imposed by the financing private sector, or to follow a long term project with a limited budget. While contributing to higher employment and an economic boom, the former policy does, however, run contrary to the ideals of an Islamic just society as advocated not only by Moussavi, but also by his critic, Montazeri. Due to its shortcomings, the latter policy is likely to alienate the government from the momentum of the revolution and, therefore, from the bulk of the population. It is also likely to distance it from the strong lobby of private sector supporters which exist in the *Majlis*, the bazaar and also amongst the ulama.

The success of Prime Minister Moussavi in putting his policies into practice without compromising on revolutionary goals or intensifying the hostility of his opponents depends on his ability to manoeuvre between the two extremes. By doing this he would secure a fusion, amidst the tension, which is of great importance to the continuity of Khomeini's reformist theory of the Islamic state. Thanks to his statesmanship, Moussavi has so far been able to enjoy Khomeini's support and maintain office in the face of the obstruction and opposition of his opponents including President Khamenei.

However, this is support that Prime Minister Moussavi cannot rely upon for long. Khomeini is old and ailing, while, with another presidential election pending, the Prime Minister is by no means sure of being reappointed to office. The question of which faction comes to power, then, is likely to depend to a great extent on the death or survival of Khomeini as well as to the power held by Rafsanjani and Montazeri at the time of the presidential election.

In addition to the charismatic qualities that Ayatollah Khomeini exhibited during the 1979 revolution, it is his jurisprudential position as *wali faqi* in the Islamic Republic's system of power that puts him above all legislation concerning political, social and economic matters as well as religious decrees, and it is this position that Ayatollah Montazeri has been designated to take over after Khomeini.

At present, however, Montazeri seems to have been shunned by a group of his opponents known for their moderate views in politics and reformist attitudes in religion, most prominently personified by Rafsanjani. The struggle between the two groups reached its peak with the Irangate scandal when Mehdi Hashemi, the brother of Ayatollah Montazeri's son-in-law, and the director of the Office for Islamic Liberation, was arrested. The office was eventually closed and the concept of exporting revolution, of which Ayatollah Montazeri was a leading advocate, suffered a setback. With the subsequent homage paid to Montazeri by Rafsanjani and Moussavi, and by Montazeri's own denunciation of Mehdi Hashemi, a reconciliation seemed to have been achieved. Meanwhile the tension continued to exist, particularly in the theological colleges of Qom and amongst the Revolutionary Guards, and gained momentum following Iran's acceptance of UN Resolution 598. Later, Ayatollah Montazeri was practically excluded from the state-controlled media and a number of ulama loyal to him were executed.

In spite of his apparent defeat, Ayatollah Montazeri continues to pose a serious threat to the pro-Rafsanjani group of politicians and their policies as well as to the continuity of Ayatollah Khomeini's Islamic line on social, political and economic issues. He may have lost some of his authority due to the change of circumstances in Iran after the end of the war, but his adherents in parliament, the bazaar and theological centres still represent a powerful lobby. Montazeri's views of the eternal quality of Islam, timeless and universalized enough to dispense with any change of reform, stands in contrast to Ayatollah Khomeini's reformist approach. Since the settlement of the war, the columns of the state-controlled media have frequently contained both testimonies to the quest for modernism, and attacks on Islamic traditionalism and the traditionalists, which in turn bear witness to a growing opposition against the religious decrees issued by Khomeini and the social and economic policies enforced by the government. The traditionalists, according to Rafsanjani, are a hindrance to government in fulfilling its programmes, because of their opposition to the redistribution of wealth and the employment of technocrats. The alienation of the theological centres from Ayatollah Khomeini's political line, whether in support of Montazeri or not, is a danger signal for the policy of state centralization and the power of the Rafsanjani group, and the prospects of continuing fusion among the leadership. It has been suggested, for instance, that the Administration of the Shrine of the eighth Shia Imam, Ali ibn Musa al-Reza, in Mashad, has been a powerful organization operating independently of the government and enforcing its own policies. The Islamic traditionalists certainly represent a strong faction in Iranian politics, utilizing an interpretation of Islamic teachings different from those of Ayatollah Khomeini, in order to oppose the government. It is apparently to this group of theologians that Khomeini refers in his letter of guidance stating that they are not qualified to have a share in running the state, as their knowledge of Islam is not combined with a good sense of social affairs.

There is no absolute guarantee that Khomeini, even if he survives the presidential election, will get his man elected. Nor is the power of Rafsanjani unchallenged. There have already been reports of three unsuccessful attempts on his life. Besides, the latest mass summary executions carried out in Iran have had great international as well as internal repercussions which are not likely to be of much help to the pro-Rafsanjani group. The issue has already been utilized by Ayatollah Montazeri, who in an open letter addressed to the Minister of Justice as well as to Ayatollah Khomeini, has questioned the theological and judicial legitimacy of the executions.

Considering all these circumstances, the possibility of a change in the balance of power in the near future should not be underestimated. Meanwhile, other opposition forces, weakened by internal divisions seem unlikely to be able to impose a serious threat to the Islamic Republic, at least for some time to come. It seems Khomeini has at least secured the continuity of the Islamic Republic after his death in spite of internal tension and regardless of which faction is likely to win. Moreover, he has tried to reincarnate himself in his son Ahmad Khomeini, who is expected to be the sole interpreter of his father's statements. Naturally Ayatollah Khomeini hopes for the continuity of the type of Islamic state created by himself. How far his hope is likely to materialize depends on the balance of power in the Islamic Republic's polarized system.

Black veils for Khomeini in Tehran (*Nick Danziger*)

Jerusalem Day—the poster marks Iran's commitment to liberate the
Holy City (*Nick Danziger*)

REPORTAGE

1. FRIDAY PRAYERS

Nick Danziger

"Revolution!" I yelled as I stood in the middle of the road in a bid to stop one of the fixed-route taxis. I was on my toes, ready to spring back to the relative safety of the pavement if the taxi wasn't ready to stop. You had no warning either way.

The taxis, like most of the cars in Tehran, are based on an old Hillman model, still rolling off the production line and called *Paykans*. To cross town effectively, you plan a route of interconnecting taxis, which really operate on the principle of buses, having a fixed journey but stopping wherever requested, and picking up whenever there's a spare seat (or even corner) according to the driver's whim. To stop one, all you have to do is stand in the middle of the screaming traffic and flag it down. It's simple, if you're brave and strong and don't set too high a value on your life, and you have to yell out your destination, because of course the taxis don't display their route, so you have to find one by trial-and-error. My destination that day was Revolution Square to watch the masses demonstrate their support for the liberation of Jerusalem. Not surprisingly, all the street names have been changed since Khomeini seized power—and all the names that bore even the remotest reference to the Pahlavi dynasty have been expunged. Tehran's Winston Churchill Avenue has been renamed after Bobby Sands, the IRA hunger-striker.

When it was possible to ignore the political climate, Tehran could be compared to a New York of the East with its regular traffic jams and helicopter traffic reports. Like New York, Tehran remains a cosmopolitan town, with many Bengalis, Sikhs, Sri Lankans, Pakistanis, and Afghans amongst others.

The city is covered with graffiti—slogans proclaiming the virtues of the revolution. Posters and placards too: stuck up, torn down, replaced, reaffixed, and notices of the deaths of the martyrs of the Gulf War. Slogans of loathing abound: "Neither West nor East!" "Liberalism:the butcher of colonialism and the steamroller of imperialism!" Huge portrait murals of the various ayatollahs, their patrician beards filling the frames. And everywhere the super-patrician Khomeini—solemn, proud and defiant: "We defend the oppressed and fight the oppressor."

On the Sabbath and on all holy days many thousands gather at Tehran University to demonstrate their solidarity with the regime. By the time I reached Revolution Avenue the crowds were already streaming towards Tehran University for prayers in the heat of the midday sun. With a portrait of Khomeini behind them, two pied pipers—a saxophonist and a clarinetist—led a group of demonstrators into the university. The road was flooded with men, on either side of it marched black-chadored columns of women. The procession gave the impression of being half-carnival, half-funeral, which indeed was something akin to the mood of the day. They came in groups, civilians of all ages—brothers, fathers, grandfathers, all waving their clenched fists in the air and shouting: *"Jang, jang ta piruzi!"* (War, war to the death!) and *"Margh barg Amerika, margh barg Israel!"* (Death to America, death to Israel!) Then followed a platoon of goose-stepping new recruits, the broad red stripes down the sides of their light khaki trousers providing a sudden splash of colour, and each with a photo of Khomeini pinned to his chest.

The crowd was slowly working itself into a frenzy. Mullahs who had taken part in the war marched past with red roses in the barrels of their machine guns. Then came another wave of civilians, chanting and beating their breasts. Then came a column of children, marching in single file. Each held a painting or a banner and a red rose of martyrdom. One eight-year-old wore army fatigues and a tin helmet with a red bandana tied round it. On one side of his chest was pinned a picture of Khomeini, on the other the insignia of the Revolutionary Guard Corps—a clenched fist holding a gun. Many children had shaved heads, and almost all of them wore a red bandana inscribed with their willingness to die for Islam: "We positively accept your cause and call to fight." Potential martyrs—marked down for the war in years to come.

In the middle of the road a solitary man sat by a vast perspex box. It was a money box, and as they passed, the crowd stuffed notes into it as their contribution to the war effort. I thought of the words of the government: that the Islamic Revolution had turned Iran "from a selfish and over-consuming state . . . into a society which is purified and generous; and this generosity is in giving everything from the smallest item to the most dear possession, that is, one's own son".

On entering Tehran University a vast ocean of thousands of worshippers including government ministers, foreign dignitaries and Iraqi POWs faced a wooden, box-like dais framed in slogans from where a robed and turbaned ayatollah was speaking. Bespectacled and severe, Ayatollah Mahdavi-Kani clutched a Kalashnikov. He addressed the crowd: "The people of the Moslem countries must unite in order to remove the Zionist tumour from the region and they should not accept aggression against their greatness . . . one billion Moslems should make a joint effort to liberate their first *Quibla* (Jerusalem)." The worshippers were choking with emotion at his words, and at one point everyone linked hands, in a wave of intoxicating solidarity.

2. REVOLUTIONARIES, THE CENTRE FOR COMBATING SIN, AND NORMAN WISDOM

Nick Danziger

The Islamic Revolution in Iran produced great changes in the arts. Anything considered un-Islamic was banned, but this has changed to a certain extent and much is now tolerated—once Ayatollah Khomeini has given his approval. Bans on music, indoor games and the televising of sporting events have been lifted or modified. However, what was and wasn't allowed during my visit to Iran was compounded by the fact that it coincided with Ramadan, the month-long sunrise-to-sunset fast.

Any defiance against Islamic laws had to be guarded, for fear of incurring the anger of the numerous self-styled guardians of public morality. I heard of a woman who had taken to razor-slashing other women whom she thought improperly dressed. Such groups as the Guards of the Mobile Units of the Wrath of God, the Centre for Combating Sin, and the *Hezbollahis* (the partisans of the Party of God), kept a close eye on public propriety. Brooding over all of these were the omnipresent Islamic Revolutionary Guards—the *Pasdaran*.

I remember a woman getting into a fixed-route taxi in tears. It was still Ramadan, and though some people sneaked meals or glasses of water in back rooms during the day, they did so at their peril. This woman's eight menfolk had been surprised by the *Pasdaran* in the middle of a meal, arrested and taken away.

There were, however, great inconsistencies. Communist literature was banned, and yet English copies of Marx and Engels were freely available. Many Iranians I met were voracious readers and copies of Dostoyevsky, Victor Hugo and Emile Zola translated into Farsi were eagerly snapped up.

The cinema posed a major problem for one of the twentieth century's most puritanical regimes. Foreign films were heavily censored and cut, but war films and thrillers which didn't feature unveiled women were everywhere. On my first visit to Tehran I opted for an Italian thriller. The cinema had all the friendly ambiance of a tube station at rush hour, people constantly coming and going irrespective of the film's progress. Of course the film had been cut to ribbons but there was one striking moment that had escaped the scissors—a woman appeared in a sleeveless cardigan. This sent the all-male audience into a state of near-hysterical excitement.

Television suffered the same fate as the cinema. Even major sports events were a problem for the authorities as they featured skimpily-clad athletes. Television films were heavily censored and I was amazed to see university students going wild over, of all things, old Norman Wisdom movies.

It was only in September 1988 that Ayatollah Khomeini gave his blessing to chess, banned at the beginning of the revolution with all other indoor games, deemed to be un-Islamic and therefore unhealthy. The sports pages of the papers exhorted people to train their children in swimming and archery.

Within months of the Islamic revolution most music was banned on the grounds of corrupting the spirit and having an indolent effect on the mind. Martial music was permitted—considered uplifting. Pop music and folksongs were outlawed. Whilst the nationwide street public address systems filled the air with a regular diet of Islamic song, revolutionary chants and dirges, television and radio broadcasts were often introduced by Western classical music, Beethoven being one of the favourites. There was also a thriving industry in the recorded speeches of the clergy, with tapes sold in shops or on upturned cartons by street vendors.

Signs of defiance were always discreet. While pop music was banned, I went to more than one party where, behind closed doors and windows, and drawn curtains, Michael Jackson was softly played and danced to. The music was so soft that if anybody talked you couldn't hear it. There were no chadors at these gatherings—men and women were together, their faces a mixture of sadness and temporary relief—a kind of unabashed delight. The partygoers drank "rocket-fuel" on the rocks—a loathsome vodka clumsily home-made from distilled raisins, but at least blissfully alcoholic.

One area that has continued to flourish under the present regime has been the fine arts. I was keen to visit Tehran's Museum of Modern Art as it had once housed one of the finest collections of twentieth-century art outside the western hemisphere. However, I was saddened but not totally surprised to see the entire priceless collection had disappeared. Only a few heavy statues, by Henry Moore and Giacometti, too awkward to remove, remained neglected in the garden, not hidden from view but emphatically not included in the exhibition. The exhibition itself was a nightmare of Iranian post-revolutionary art: a sort of debased surrealism obsessed with blood and death, and crude political propaganda. "Martyrs' City" was vaguely reminiscent of Magritte: only his clouds were replaced by floating shrouded corpses. In another, a barefooted, chadored woman stands on a windswept hill holding a gun from whose muzzle a rose, the symbol of martyrdom, extends. Wrapped in the folds of her chador at her back, a baby sleeps: a mixture of belligerence and cloying sentimentality. Yet another depicts Jesus fleeing from a shirtsleeved Mr Hyde, on whose chest are tattooed a gun, a Star of David and a whisky bottle. The message of the painting is inscribed in English: "While running away Jesus said: 'An ignorant man is coming'."

Most of the paintings were figurative—unusual in Islamic art and indeed proscribed by the Koran. I asked one of the artists about this apparent anomaly:

"You will notice that the figures are not well painted," he said. This was indeed true—they have been compared to a throwback to primitive Christian representations of saints. "This is deliberate. Minor faults are intentional because only God can create perfection."

So, man has to be deliberately imperfect, I wondered, but did not say.

3.   A VIEW FROM THE MORGUE

Amit Roy

It is midnight at the morgue as two trucks arrive straight from Tehran airport with 37 rough, wooden coffins. These contain the latest batch of bodies from the 300 or so Iranian pilgrims killed in Mecca, Islam's holiest shrine, in a clash with Saudi police in July 1987.

"The Tehran morgue is always a busy place," says the gatekeeper, standing by a poster depicting a typically-Iranian concept of war and peace—a dove sipping from a pool of blood.

Revolutionary Guards whip off the Iranian flags covering the coffins, scoop up armfuls of gladioli that had earlier been placed on top and drop them into a large pitcher of water. The flowers will be used again since more coffins are expected on later flights.

The guards begin prising open the coffin lids with crowbars. One of the morgue attendants pulls on a pair of yellow washing-up gloves of the sort sold in any supermarket and prepares to display the dead.

It is almost a cliché to observe that death has become a way of life in revolutionary Iran. But certainly the celebration of violent death, when it occurs in the pursuit of an approved cause, has become an integral part of the nation's Shia revolutionary culture. There are worse places to start trying to understand Ayatollah Khomeini's philosophy than the morgue—*Pezeshk-e-ghanooni* (legal medical centre)—in Tehran's *Park-e-Shah* district. The arrivals at the morgue tell the story of post-revolutionary Iran.

The body of Gen. Nematollah Nassiri, head of SAVAK, the Shah's feared secret police and the symbol of all that was wrong with the previous regime, was brought here after he was summarily executed shortly after the revolution on Feb.12, 1979.

Photographers were invited to a "photocall" at the morgue to take pictures of Nassiri and three others executed with him—the governors of Tehran and Isfahan and a paratroop commander—in half-opened refrigerator drawers. These lasting images from the morgue were then flashed around the world by the international news agencies.

"This is just the start of the executions," pledged Iran's new masters, and they proved true to their word.

After a huge bomb demolished the Tehran headquarters of the clergy-dominated Islamic Republican Party in June 1981, the bodies of Ayatollah Beheshti, arguably Iran's most influential clergyman at the time after Khomeini, and 70 of the country's most senior politicians were dug out from the rubble under the glare of television lights.

"They were all brought here," recalls the morgue gatekeeper, with the pride of a man whose clientele has resembled almost a *Who's Who* of revolutionary figures.

However, not all the arrivals have been famous. During the Gulf War, each offensive meant the arrival of hundreds of bodies at the Tehran morgue. Often, they had to be piled up in the stinking heat of the courtyard, since all available cold storage space inside was taken.

Najumul Hassan, a Reuters correspondent, arrived from Delhi in 1983 to cover the war and was killed two days later in Bakhtaran when shrapnel pierced his head. A friend who went to collect his body from the morgue first had to rummage through a mountain of dead.

Morgue officials were baffled by the fuss over one victim. "So many others have been martyred," they said, "Why worry about one body?"

Even before the revolution, the morgue became a stopping-off point for bodies on their journey to Behesht-e-Zahra, the sprawling cemetery on the edges of south Tehran, where demonstrators shot by the Shah's soldiers lie buried.

Little has changed at the morgue, where now the attendant with the yellow gloves is busy unwrapping the latest arrivals from Mecca. The figures resemble waxworks from the London Dungeon, except that their names are scrawled on the sides of the coffins in Farsi with black felt-tip pen.

Two of the bodies have small holes in the chest; another in the back; and on an elderly man with a white beard there is a big gap where his right ear should be. The attendant squeezes a yellow-gloved finger into another wound to drive home his point. What caused the holes are judgments better left to forensic experts but even the untrained eye can scarcely fail to notice the clawing fingers frozen in the moment of death.

The gatekeeper is unperturbed at the prospect of more arrivals. "We are prepared to receive more martyrs," he says casually. "Yes," agrees one of his friends, "the nation would like that".

4. AT THE COURT OF KHOMEINI

Amit Roy

The Iranian air force officers look like strong men, immaculate in their blue uniforms even though some have arrived straight from the war front after flying sorties against the Iraqis. But their reaction as Ayatollah Khomeini enters the mosque, hand raised in silent greeting, is unexpected: they burst out weeping. It is Feb.8, 1981; early morning in Jamaran, the village where Khomeini lives, tucked away in the Alborz mountains to the north of Tehran.

Khomeini's son, Ahmad, brought him here in February, 1980, from the holy but dusty city of Qom after his father suffered a mild heart attack and needed a healthier environment. The choice is wise: the air in posh Jamaran is 5–7° C cooler and a lot cleaner than in Khomeini's natural constituency—bustling, working-class south Tehran. For security and health reasons, Khomeini no longer goes to the people. The people come to him.

Among those who have arrived to see Khomeini today are a group of widows, whose husbands have been killed at the front. The war with Iraq has been raging since September 1980, and casualties are mounting.

To get into Jamaran is a daunting business. Layer upon layer of security is provided by thousands of zealous revolutionary guards who have encouraged local residents to "donate" their houses to Khomeini's entourage.

The morning sun lights up the labyrinth of lanes in Jamaran, as the women are herded into the local *hosseinieh*—a small mosque—to await the Ayatollah's arrival. Along Niavaran Road, which winds past the late Shah's winter palace, come the marching air force officers. They, too, crowd expectantly into the mosque for they have come to mark a significant anniversary.

Two years previously, on Feb.8, 1979, a group of air force officers met Khomeini shortly after his return home from 15 years' exile and pledged their loyalty to him. The meeting took place at the Refah girls' school in central Tehran where Khomeini had established his headquarters.

A photograph which appeared in *Ettelaat*, a Tehran daily, showing the officers saluting Khomeini, was dismissed by the authorities as a fake since the men had their faces hidden from camera. But fake it was not.

The crucial support given by the air force to Khomeini was the catalyst which persuaded other sections of the armed forces also to defect, and triggered the revolution 48 hours later.

Today, 1,000 air force officers—a different lot from the group in 1979—wait in the mosque which is connected by a private passage to Khomeini's villa. His routine is to rise early for prayers, listen to overseas radio news—perhaps Voice of America, the BBC's Farsi service or even Israel—and glance through an Iranian news agency summary.

By and by, the steel doors linking the passage to the mosque slide open, and revolutionary guards and assorted clergymen file in and line up on a raised balcony. Next comes Khomeini's son, Ahmad, who is to become his father's link with the outside world. He positions himself by an empty peacock-blue armchair. Only then, looking frail but walking unaided, his pale, unsmiling face contrasting with his dark cloak, does Khomeini emerge.

Pandemonium breaks out and pro-Khomeini slogans fill the mosque. The air force officers, remembering times past and overcome by emotion, weep hysterically. But not a flicker crosses Khomeini's face.

With the air force chief, Col. Javad Fakhouri, by his side, Khomeini tells the audience: "This day, two years ago, you decided to come and see me and join your brothers." He adds in colloquial Farsi: "That was a great day in history, and in the history of the air force. All the other forces followed your example."

He advises the armed forces to steer clear of political controversy, a reference to rumours that President Abolhassan Bani-Sadr is trying to win them over in his power struggle against the hardline clergy. Later, Bani-Sadr, once dubbed "Khomeini's spiritual son", would be dismissed as president and flee the country.

Among other changes, the security in Jamaran will get tighter with anti-aircraft guns mounted on Khomeini's heavily-fortified villa. Revolutionary guards will isolate the Imam, block all roads into the village, ban the public from a nearby park and forbid movement on ski slopes overlooking Khomeini's house.

It is to this village that Khomeini would be confined, where he would meet his ministers and key clergymen and pronounce periodically, oracle-like, on matters of war and peace. But all that is in the future.

This morning, a war widow emerges, strangely comforted, from a private audience with Khomeini. She clutches a child in one arm and, in a gesture characteristically Iranian, a large photograph of her husband. She has been moved by a kindly aspect of Khomeini that will remain hidden to the outside world.

But what did Khomeini say?

"Oh, nothing very much," she says, "but I feel better".

5.   IRANIAN DISSONANCE

Vahe Petrossian

One of the more surprising realities of revolutionary Iran is the enthusiasm and abandon with which people in Tehran and elsewhere voice their dissatisfaction with the government, or just simply grumble. No leader, not even Khomeini, is too sacrosanct to be openly criticized—and without apparent fear of retribution.

The expressions of public dissatisfaction continued through the most sensitive periods of the Gulf War, when the government had every excuse to clamp down. Only in the repressive year or so after the June 1981 confrontation between the government and the ousted President Bani-Sadr and the *Mujaheddin* guerrillas, did Iranians revert to their Shah-era habit of looking over their shoulders before voicing political opinions in public.

Lively discussions take place everywhere from the public street to the privacy of the home, although arbitrariness in official behaviour and the enforcement of laws lends a nervous edge to daily life, particularly for women who have to observe Islamic dress regulations in public. Middle-class women, for example, can usually get away with loose headscarves and with showing a little leg, but they never know when the roving *komiteh* personnel—the revolutionary police—will decide to take offence and pull them in for a lecture or a lashing. Ten years after the revolution, there is still a feeling that one could get arrested for no good reason, perhaps even jailed or executed without a proper hearing.

The high levels of popular criticism reflect both the divisions within Iranian society and the relatively tolerant attitude of the Islamic clergy. While the revolutionary authorities have been quick to resort to harsh repression of opposition activity, they are not as a rule over-sensitive to generalized criticism.

Foreign correspondents can feel this almost from the moment they set foot in Tehran. The airport taxi driver usually needs no prompting to launch into a critique of everything that is wrong with the regime. The communal taxis—shared by up to four passengers—provide an ideal venue for heated political debate. Complete strangers discuss everything from high prices to the conduct of the war and the perfidy of the "mullahs"—a term for the clergy which is often used in a derogatory tone. In contrast to neighbouring countries, correspondents have little trouble getting comments from ordinary people and officials alike. As often as not, the opinions expressed are critical.

"Peace? What peace? Nothing will change until the mullahs are changed!" was one Iranian's response to a question about his hopes for the future. "They've ruined this country", says a taxi passenger, "you can't have fun any more; you can't drink or go out; all we have left is to sit at home and watch bearded creatures on television". Queues at shops are favourite places for heaping loud abuse on the government and exchanging the latest rumours, or reports from Israel Radio, the Voice of America or the BBC.

It is not unusual to hear even Khomeini—often referred to as "that old man"—being blamed or berated on the streets of Tehran. This was particularly noticeable after the peace agreement with Iraq. Opponents of the government wanted to know why "that old man" had not accepted a settlement earlier, when Iran still held the upper hand in the conflict. Bearded *Hezbollah* types without a ready answer found themselves the object of much teasing.

Iranians' tendency to express their opinions is far from properly reflected in the official and semi-official media. State radio and television stick to the government line, although newspapers are freer to question and to criticize. There is, however, an increasing audience for books, the censorship of which is relatively lax. In contrast to pre-revolution days, Iranians have become voracious readers of historical books and political and social novels. Pre-1979, a print run of 5,000 was exceptional for any book, whereas now first editions of 20,000 are not unusual.

REFERENCE SECTION

POPULATION

Total population in the 1986 census was recorded as 49,857,384. Growth rate during 1987 was estimated as 2.8 per cent per annum. Average life expectancy is 59 years. The principal population centres are as follows (figures from the 1986 census):

Tehran	6,022,029
Mashad	1,500,000
Isfahan	1,000,000

Other major towns with a population in excess of 500,000 are Tabriz, Shiraz, Bakhtaran, Karaj and Ahwaz.

ECONOMIC ACTIVITY

INDUSTRY AND AGRICULTURE

Iran's principal industry is oil production. During 1987, it produced an average of 2,250,000 barrels per day. Total recoverable oil reserves were estimated by the National Iranian Oil Company to total 93,000 million barrels.

Other extractive industries include coal, salt, iron, copper and zinc ore mining. Leading non-petroleum products include cement, paints, refined sugar, vehicle assembly, cigarettes and household goods.

Principal crops are wheat, sugar-beet, sugar-cane, potatoes and rice. The main livestock products are milk, eggs, poultry, mutton/lamb and beef/veal.

EXTERNAL TRADE

Iran's leading exports (other than petroleum) are fruit (fresh and dried) and carpets. Principal imports include machinery and transport equipment, basic manufactured goods, chemicals and chemical products, and foodstuffs. Its main trading partners are as follows:

Imports	1987 trade in US$ million
West Germany	1,575.4
Japan	1,043.0
Italy	505.6
United Kingdom	505.0

Exports

United States	1,751.5
Japan	1,556.0
Italy	1,047.5
Turkey	948.0

Iran's current account balance-of-payments surplus for 1987–88 was estimated as totalling some US$1,000 million, in contrast to a deficit of US$3,500 million the previous year. As of mid-1988, Iran's total debt to industrialized countries (including both banks and official trade credits) amounted to US$4,087 million.

POLITICAL STRUCTURE

THE CONSTITUTION

The Constitution enshrines the concept of an Islamic Republic, in which the teachings of Islam provide the basis for the political, economic and social conduct of the state and the people. Overall authority is vested in the *wali faqi*, the country's spiritual leader, currently Ayatollah Khomeini, whose successor is nominated by an elected Assembly of Experts, composed of 83 clergy. If no individual emerges, the Assembly may choose a council of leadership of three or five persons. In all cases, the choice must meet with the approval of the nation. Legislative, executive and judicial power are all under the ultimate authority of the *wali faqi*, who is also Supreme Commander of the armed forces, including the Revolutionary Guard. He approves all candidates to the Presidency, and can dismiss the President on the basis of a no-confidence vote in the *Majlis* or a decision of the Supreme Court.

For practical purposes, executive power is vested in the President, and legislative authority in a 270-member Islamic Consultative Assembly (*Majlis*). Both elected by universal adult suffrage every four years. The *Majlis* must approve all members of the Council of Ministers. A 12-member Council of Guardians (comprising six religious lawyers appointed by the *wali faqi* and six lawyers appointed by the Supreme Judicial Council and approved by the *Majlis*) ensures that all legislation conforms with the Constitution and Islamic principles. The Council also has the power to veto candidates to high elected office on the same grounds.

The Constitution provides for equality between the sexes on the basis of Islamic principles. All of Iran's ethnic groups are to be accorded fair and equal treatment. The press is free subject to restrictions on publishing material which offends public morality or insults religious faith. Freedom of association, including the right to form political parties, is guaranteed, providing that no organization runs counter to the principles of independence, freedom and national unity under Islam.

THE GOVERNMENT

As of the beginning of January 1989, the government was composed as follows:

Head of state: Hojatolislam Seyed Ali Khamenei, President

Spiritual leader of Iran (*wali faqi*): Ayatollah Ruhollah Khomeini

Designated successor: Ayatollah Hossein Ali Montazeri

Speaker of the *Majlis;* Commander-in-Chief of the Armed Forces (acting): Hojatolislam Hashemi Ali Akbar Rafsanjani

Members of the Council of Ministers

Mr Hossein Moussavi	Prime Minister
Dr Ali Akbar Vellayati	Foreign Affairs
Mr Gholamreza Agazadeh	Oil
Hojatolislam Ali Akbar Mohtashemi	Interior
Mr Muhammad Javad Iravani	Economic Affairs and Finance
Mr Isa Kalantari	Agriculture and Rural Affairs
(vacant)	Commerce
Mr Namdar Zanganeh	Energy
Mr Mohammed Saeedi Kya	Roads and Transport
Mr Gholamreza Foruzesh	*Jihad* ("crusade") for Reconstruction
Mr Behzad Nabavi	Heavy Industries
Mr Gholam Reza Shafei	Industry
Mr Sarajuddin Kazeruni	Housing and Urban Development
Mr Abolqasem Sarhadizadeh	Labour and Social Affairs
Mr Mohammed Gharazi	Posts, Telephones and Telegraphs
Dr Ali Reza Marandi	Health, Treatment and Medical Education
Mr Mohammad Ali Najati	Education and Training
Dr Mohammed Farhadi	Higher Education and Culture
Mr Hassan Ebrahim Habibi	Justice
Mr Ali Shamkhani	Islamic Revolutionary Guards Corps
Hojatolislam Mohammad Mohammadi Reyshahri	Intelligence and Security

Dr Seyyed Mohammad Khatami   Culture and Islamic Guidance
Mr Massoud Zanjani   Plan and Budget Organization
Brig.-Gen. Mohammad Hussein Jalali Defence
Mr Muhammad Reza Ayatollahi   Mines and Metals

DISSIDENT ORGANIZATIONS

Left-wing movements

Communist Party of Iran (CPI) Founded in 1983 by a number of Marxist groups opposed to the pro-Soviet Tudeh Party, among them the *Komaleh* (Kurdish Communist Party of Iran—see below). Leadership: Abdullah Mohtadeh.

Fedayeen-e Khalq (People's Fighters) This militant Marxist-oriented guerrilla group staged numerous attacks against the Shah's regime. It initially supported the Islamic revolution, but subsequently denounced the government for failing to introduce full democracy. Its members clashed with revolutionary guards on several occasions in late 1979 and early 1980. After the outbreak of the war with Iraq, the *Fedayeen* leadership called for support for the defence effort, but subsequently came to oppose the war. By the mid-1980s, its activities were largely restricted exiled opposition.

Mujaheddin-e Khalq (People's Holy Warriors) This left-leaning Islamic movement played a major role in opposing the Shah and working for the Islamic revolution. From mid-1979 onwards, however, it gradually became disenchanted with the regime, clashing with fundamentalist groups and supporting President Bani-Sadr against the clerical leadership. From mid-1981 they moved into open opposition, fighting an unsuccessful armed struggle which involved the assassination of many of the regime's key figures. Widespread repression and executions effectively destroyed the *Mujaheddin* threat by 1984. From 1981 to 1986, the movement's leadership was in exile in Paris; in June 1986 they moved to Iraq, from where the group's "National Liberation Army" staged an ultimately unsuccessful drive into central Iran in the wake of the wave of Iraqi victories in mid-1988. Leadership: Massoud Rajavi.

Tudeh (People's Party) Founded in 1920 as the Communist Party of Iran, it was banned in 1931 and forced to continue its work illegally. In 1941 it was reorganized as the Tudeh Party, which was itself repressed and declared illegal in 1949. The Party welcomed the Islamic revolution as "anti-imperialist and democratic"; while again allowed to operate, it became increasingly opposed to the growing fundamentalist trend of the government. Most of its leading activists were arrested, and in May 1983 the Party was officially proscribed. A number of its leaders being subsequently executed. The Party continues to operate from the Soviet Union and East Germany. Leadership: Ali Khavari.

Moderate opposition

Association for the Defence of Freedom and Sovereignty of the Iranian Nation This moderate opposition grouping was formed in March 1986 by former Prime Minister Dr Mehdi Bazargan, leader of the Freedom Movement (see below). Seven members of Bazargan's 1979 provisional government are on the Association's central committee. It has similar aims to those of the Freedom Movement, supporting the revolutionary constitution but opposed to the war with Iraq. It has attracted harassment from radical factions.

Freedom Movement (Nelzat-Azadi) Founded by Dr Bazargan after he had resigned as Prime Minister, the Freedom Movement is the foremost remaining legal opposition group in Iran. It has repeatedly called for freedom of the press, speech and assembly, and criticized economic mismanagement. The Movement was strongly opposed to Iran's refusal to end the Gulf War after driving the Iraqis off Iranian soil. Dr Bazargan claimed that this was against the teachings of the Koran. He registered as a candidate for the presidential elections in 1985, but was rejected by the Council of Guardians.

National Council of Resistance for Liberty and Independence The NCR was set up in Paris in 1981 as an opposition alliance by the *Mujaheddin* leader, Massoud Rajavi, and ex-President Bani-Sadr, who was named as head of the NCR's "provisional government". However, Bani-Sadr subsequently left the alliance in 1984 after disagreements with Rajavi over the latter's willingness to work with Iraq. Another member group, the Kurdish Democratic Party of Iran (see below) was expelled in 1985 on the grounds that it was prepared to negotiate with the government.

National Resistance Movement Founded in Paris in 1980 by Dr Shapour Bakhtiar, the Shah's last Prime Minister, the NRM supports the principle of a liberal, constitutional monarchy, along the lines set down in the 1907 constitution. In September 1984, the Movement claimed responsibility for a bomb attack on a Revolutionary Guards' office in Tehran. In general, however, it has eschewed violence.

Reza Pahlavi (the Shah's son) and his supporters have also called for a return to a constitutional monarchy, with himself as Shah.

Kurdish groups

Komaleh (Kurdish Communist Party of Iran) Founded in 1969, the Marxist-oriented *Komaleh* waged a guerrilla struggle against the Shah's government and the Khomeini regime. It periodically co-operated with the more moderate Kurdish Democratic Party of Iran.

Kurdish Democratic Party of Iran The KDPI was formed after the Second World War out of an Association for the Resurrection of Kurdistan. From the start an illegal organization, the KDPI was virtually wiped out when a Kurdish rebellion was crushed in 1966–67. After the revolution, the group was legalized and presented its autonomy demands to the Bazargan government, but little progress had been made before heavy fighting broke out between Kurds and Revolutionary Guards in March 1979. The KDP was formally banned in August. After the outbreak of the Gulf War, the Party's *Pesh Merga* ("Forward to Death!") guerrillas began to receive substantial support from Iraq. Fighting continued over the ensuing years, with the government forces gradually gaining control of more areas as advances into Iraq deprived the *Pesh Merga* of Iraqi support. The KDPI joined the National Council of Resistance in 1981, but was expelled four years later, ostensibly because of its apparent willingness to negotiate with the Tehran authorities.

INDEX